Pierre Toussaint

A Citizen of Old New York

PIERRE TOUSSAINT
1766–1853

Pierre Toussaint

A Citizen of Old New York

By

Arthur and Elizabeth Odell Sheehan

HILLSIDE EDUCATION

Cover and interior book design by Mary Jo Loboda

Cover image: Pierre Toussaint (ca. 1781-1853), gift of Miss Georgina Schuyler, Courtesy of the New York State Historical Society. Used by permission of The Picture Art Collection / Alamy Stock Photo

Back cover: St. Peter's Church on Barclay St. NY (public domain), courtesy of WIkimedia

ISBN: 978-1-7331383-9-0

Hillside Education
475 Bidwell Hill Road
Lake Ariel, PA 18436
www.hillsideeducation.com

CONTENTS

Pierre Toussaint

Prologue

What a man is, God alone knows.

We see only what he does, and how he looks when he does it. We hear what others say about him. The rest is mystery. If ever a man was mysterious, Pierre Toussaint was. From what we can see, there is no accounting for him.

Who his forefathers were, or when the bond of slavery was laid upon them and they were led out of Africa, we do not know. From the time their bare feet touched the wet white sands of the Indies (the same sands that the navigator Columbus had once kissed in gratitude), they were strangers, and subject to the white master.

He, the master, was a Frenchman, and his fields were waiting. Heavy with their harvests of coffee and sugar they lay in the hot Caribbean sun and waited for the slave's strong hands to strip them and make the master rich.

Pierre Toussaint came of those people whose silence was broken only in the distant hills by the drumbeats at night and the wild dancing. By a curious twist of history, he was brought out of his dark tropic past and from the lush brilliance of the Antilles into the cool fresh morning light of the new republic in North America. To please his master, he learned the hairdresser's trade.

Soon sorrow and destitution came to the once wealthy household. Only Toussaint's earnings supported them. For him the situation held no irony. In the years of sickness and bitter disillusion that followed, his faith, his gaiety stayed them.

Others learned of his wisdom and generosity. He contrived his charities in silence, often with humor, always with tact. But his works spoke of him. And a legend grew.

"Go to Toussaint," people would say. "He will help. He knows what to do."

And so he lived, a long time, understanding what others could not, loving what they would not. Afterward his name was spoken with an odd reverence. New York had not known another like him. . .

A strange story.

Chapter 1

Saint Marc, 1773

The Caribbean sun blazed brightly on a September morning, as the doors of the church swung back in a burst of triumphant music and people began hurrying out. The solemn high Mass, central event of the week in the town of Saint Marc in the French colony of Saint-Domingue, was over.

The doors folded against the white stone walls of the church, hiding the royal decrees nailed to them. They were old ones anyway, and everyone who could read had read them. Besides, the West Indian subjects of Louis XV, King of France, Count of Navarre, and Lord of Lands Beyond the Seas, found little to interest them in the edicts that had come out from Paris under the great seal of yellow wax.

Everyone in the crowd had more important concerns on a Sunday morning. To the planters the Mass was not only a religious but a social event, a relief from the week-long ennui of life on the isolated plantations. To the slaves, even though many were not allowed to go to church, Sunday was a blessed day of rest from the backbreaking labor of cane and coffee field. Since before dawn they had been coming into town along all the hilly roads that led down from the surrounding countryside, for Sunday was also market day in Saint-Domingue.

"*Maman, Maman.*" A shrill voice rose above the boisterous talk. A small boy could be seen darting here and there through the crowd.

"Here, son." A tall young black woman stepped forward quickly. She grasped the child's hand and steered him firmly away from the people. "After this, Pierre, don't run away from me. Then you won't get lost."

The child did not hear the rebuke. As the crowd thinned a bit, he began to dance, keeping beside his mother with small capering steps, all eyes for the bustling activities around them.

Pierre was a slave child, his dark features showing plainly his Congo ancestry. In Saint-Domingue a man's fortune depended largely on the color of his face. White for the wealthy French plantation owners. Black for the slaves. And in between, faces of many dusky hues belonging to those of mixed blood, the *gens de couleur,* neither slaves nor aristocrats.

"This way now, Pierre." Ursule drew her son by one arm toward a handsome carriage waiting before the church rectory. Madame Bérard, their mistress, was just getting in. A coachman in a bright red jacket held open the door of the elegant equipage that had been polished and shined for its Sunday trip into town.

Down the street other carriages, more or less luxurious, were beginning to move toward the valley of the L'Artibonite where the rich plantations lay. The Rue de l'Eglise and the side streets nearby were lined with still other carriages, their horses and coachmen poised for momentary departure.

But the planters were in no hurry to get started. Back home, it would be a dull day. Here one could exchange greetings and catch up on the latest news. They stood in leisurely groups, the men in their long-tailed coats with the shiny buttons, their gold watches glinting in the noonday brightness. Most of them wore high hats and their hair in perukes, fastened with black silk ribbon. The women were dressed in rich muslins, elaborately fashioned, with huge sleeves and frills of lace. The clear tropical sun accented without flattery their pale faces.

"*Bon jour, bon jour,* Ursule." Madame Bérard spoke in French instead of the customary Creole—a sign of special affection. Ursule had been her personal maid almost as long as either could remember.

"Good day, Madame."

Ursule bent quickly to adjust the richly-upholstered cushions of the carriage seat. The road to L'Artibonite was rough and could give the carriage riders a wicked jolt now and then.

"And how is Pierre today?" Madame Bérard smiled warmly at the little boy, for even in a household where all slaves were treated with kindness Pierre was bound to be the favorite. His merry disposition, his willingness to help, even his pranks pleased her. He was only seven years old, and not yet obliged to work, but she found herself thinking of excuses to have him around the house most of the time.

"Oh, thank you, Madame, I'm well," the boy answered. He looked up expectantly. Already he was smelling the wonderful things that were cooking on the little braziers over at the marketplace.

Madame Bérard laughed. "I know, you're thinking of all

those sugar and coconut cakes you'll be eating later on." She opened her embroidered purse and handed him a coin. "Now mind, don't make yourself sick!"

"Thank you, thank you, Madame." Pierre jumped up and down in his excitement.

Madame Bérard turned to Ursule.

"Why not take Pierre over to the new theater on La Grande Rue for the afternoon performance? Volange is playing, and our little mimic here ought to like that." Volange had been the rage of Paris, and as Pierre, a born imitator, often amused everyone at the plantation with his comic impersonations, his mistress' suggestion was not without self-interest.

Ursule hesitated. "Thank you, Madame, that is very kind, but . . ."

"There are seats in back for you and Pierre," Madame Bérard explained, seeing the slave woman's doubt. The mistress was quite familiar with the arrangement of the new theater, for the Bérards had a great interest in it, and had contributed generously to the new building. They hoped it would mean a new beginning for theatrical entertainment in Saint Marc. The people needed to forget the dreadful happenings of the earthquake three years ago. On that terrible evening of June 3, 1770, *Cartouche* was being given in a building temporarily rented for theatricals when a violent tremor had caused the stage to collapse and had sent the spectators screaming into the street. After that, and until the new theater was built, performances had been given from time to time in the open air, and at the mercy of sudden tropical rainstorms.

Ursule smiled as she recalled an unfortunate experience. "Madame no doubt remembers the time it rained all during the play, and I tried to hold the umbrella over her and Mademoiselle De Pointe?"

Madame Bérard laughed. "Between the rain and the wobbling umbrella we saw little of *that* performance," she said crisply. Then, as she settled back in the seat of the carriage, she added, "But speaking of De Pointe—I had a long letter from my daughter yesterday."

"I hope all is well with them in Paris," said Ursule quickly, for she knew that mail from abroad had been received at the plantation on the day before when she had been down at the river washing. She was thinking not only of the Bérard children, but of her own mother Zénobie who for the second time had made the voyage with them to Paris. There were the three girls, Victoire, Félicité, Eulalie, De Pointe's sisters, and Lester, Du Pithon and Des Glajeux, her brothers, besides Jean Jacques, the oldest, who would one day be master of the plantation.

"Yes, thank God, all the children are in good health." Madame Bérard seemed lost in her own thoughts as she continued, "Sometimes I feel that with so many of my family in Paris, my husband and I should be there too. Perhaps some day when Jean Jacques has finished his studies . . ."

The boy Pierre had been listening eagerly, and now he voiced the question on Ursule's own lips as he eagerly put in:

"And Gran'mère, is she in good health too?"

"Zénobie is very well, Pierre. When she has De Pointe settled in school she will soon be back with us. Of course, De Pointe is a little lonely just now. She says she misses the plantation and her mother—yes, and you too, Pierre, her little playmate."

"I wish Mademoiselle De Pointe were back. I miss her too," said Pierre, a shade of sadness coming over his bright face.

"So do I, Pierre," his mistress said. "I miss all the children so much! But they must have an education, and there is no place to obtain that here."

It was true. The shops of Saint-Domingue were filled with the very latest in Parisian fashions, rich laces, exquisite gowns. Those of Saint Marc did not compare with the luxury-filled stores of the capital city to the north—Cap Français, known as "the Paris of the Antilles." But still the marts that lined Saint Marc's stone-paved plaza, facing the small, blue, pouch-shaped bay, were filled with elegancies of every kind. The town, because of its climate, had become a popular watering place for the wealthy families of the colony.

Still, it lacked the schools and colleges that the rich merchants and aristocrats demanded for their children. Three-quarters of a century after its acquisition by France, Saint-Domingue was still a pioneer colony, fabulously rich, but lacking in cultural advantages. It was the custom of the French planters to stay in the Indies only till their fortune was made—sometimes it took only the short space of three years—and then to return to their native land to enjoy their wealth.

Monsieur Bérard had broken away from a group of friends in front of the church and was coming toward the waiting carriage at his wife's signal.

"How's my big boy today?" he said as he put his arm briefly around Pierre's shoulder before stepping into his seat.

"Madame says I may take him to the theater," said Ursule.

"To the theater! Well, now, I suppose he'll be leaving us to join the actors." Monsieur Bérard liked to joke with Pierre, to make him laugh and hear his quick answers. "Maybe we'll see you there. We too will stop there before we go back to L'Artibonite."

The coachman closed the carriage door and climbed up to

the driver's seat. A flurry of white dust rose from the unpaved street as the carriage swept down the Rue de l'Eglise and turned into the Rue Bourbon several blocks away.

"*Maman*." Pierre looked after it, his face suddenly sober. "Why did De Pointe have to go to Paris? We used to play every day and have so much fun."

Not much older than Pierre, De Pointe was not only his playmate, but also his godmother. Pierre had been happy when he wove for her little arbors of magnolia and palm leaves, and she would sit beneath them, protected from the hot sun, and play the grand lady. The boy would run back and forth bringing her gifts of fruit and flowers. Now, with De Pointe far away in a place called France, loneliness had come to Pierre's world, the plantation.

Ursule did not always pay much attention to Pierre's questions. There were so many of them, and she was often preoccupied. Just now she was thinking of the new kerchief she would buy when they went over to the market.

"Why does she, *Maman?*" the boy insisted.

"Oh, she's going to be a young lady in society and talk to the young gentlemen all about what's going on in the world," answered Ursule absently.

"But can't she go to school right here in Saint Marc? Then she could teach me to read and write words too."

Pierre's craving for knowledge was something Ursule did not care to encourage. She herself had never learned to read or write and she saw no reason why her son, destined for the life of a slave, should worry himself over such things.

She spoke sternly. "Now, Pierre, don't you bother your head with such ideas. Reading books is all right for white people, not for you. You just be a good boy and learn your prayers and never mind the books."

"But Gran'mère Zénobie can do it. She taught me to write my name. And some day—" determination made him speak, for once, quite slowly— "some day I'm going to read all those books Monsieur Bérard has in his room, the ones he brought from France."

Ursule was sometimes just a little troubled over him. Pierre was so full of will and spirit. It would not do for a slave child to have ambitions that were only for the rich whites.

They were turning the corner now, across from the church, and walking toward the Place d'Armes, the huge square and marketplace of Saint Marc. It was especially crowded this Sunday.

The slaves made the scene gay, for they loved bright colors, and their clothing, although made of the cheapest cotton, had all the brilliance of the tropical countryside. Purple from the omnipresent bougainvillea vine, yellow from the fragrant mimosa, green from the palms that swayed endlessly above them, vivid blue from the Caribbean sky, flashing red from the languid hibiscus flower.

There were also many of the *gens de couleur* in the crowd, but such primitive attire was not for them. Their mixed ancestry raised them socially far above the slaves. Indeed many had become rich and owned slaves themselves. But the laws of the colony, dictated by fear, forbade them to dress like the whites. They were undoubtedly potential rivals, and their increasing power and numbers made the French aristocrats uneasy. On the other hand if the elaborately dressed white women, coming from church on Sunday, looked enviously at the beautiful mulatto girls, they could say nothing. They had long since learned to accept this threat as the price of a fortune in sugar or coffee that would support them royally in

France during their declining years.

On every side was the noise and bustle of the peddlers and merchants, hawking their fruits and dry goods and vegetables in the lanes lining the four sides of the square. Slaves went past, expertly balancing on their heads huge baskets of wares for the market. There were a few white people—the soldiers from the casern in their cocked hats and long tunics, the King's sailors on leave from the men-of-war, sporting their cockades, pea jackets, buckled shoes and quaint "petticoat" trousers. Pierre also saw a few sailors in an outfit he had learned to recognize as coming from the Thirteen Colonies to the north. They were arriving in Saint-Domingue these days in greater numbers than ever before. English and French conversation mingled with the softer Creole, that strange tongue born in the tropics out of the sheer necessity of communication among slaves brought from many different parts of Africa and who knew no common language.

The town of Saint Marc, nestling against the mountains, with its blue, white, pink and other brightly colored houses set like jewels in greenery, was not a big place. Only two-thirds of a mile long and a third of a mile in width, one could walk its length and breadth in a short time. The streets bore traditional names such as Rue Dauphine, Rue Bourbon, Rue Royale, Saint-Charles, Saint-Simon and Saint-Germain, attesting to two streams of thought, royal and religious. The long avenues, running north and south over the waters of the Saint Marc River, had names one might find in any seaport —Rue Neuve, de l'Eglise, de la Marine and La Grande Rue.

Many of the buildings were handsome works of architecture, often built of stone quarried in the hills that lined the crescent-shaped bay of Saint Marc. Pierre looked admiringly at the houses around the square, and then stopped suddenly before a market stall to say:

"Oh, *Maman,* look—the cakes! I want one of these, and these!" Each delicacy looked more tempting. It was hard for a small, hungry child to choose. He tightly clutched the coin Madame Bérard had given him and scanned the sweets with a practiced eye.

Finally, a cake in each hand, he permitted Ursule to lead him away from the marketplace down to the water's edge. They sat there a while with Pierre munching his cakes, watching the high-masted ships riding at anchor along the shore, waiting for their cargoes of barreled sugar, molasses, rum, coffee and other produce.

After a time, they got up and wandered leisurely up La Grande Rue toward the theater, Pierre chattering excitedly about the actors he would see that afternoon. When they arrived at the theater it was almost time for the play to begin.

For weeks to come Madame Bérard was to reap the reward of her indulgence, for Pierre enlivened the evenings at the plantation with impersonations of Volange and the other actors he had seen that day in Saint Marc.

CHAPTER 2

THE PLANTATION

In those days the valley of L'Artibonite in the middle region of Saint-Domingue, where the plantation of the Bérard family lay, was a rich meadowland, surrounded by mountains with such picturesque names as Morne du Diable and Morne La Selle. The island originally called by the natives, Haiti—mountainous land—was itself a mountain rising dramatically from the sea. In Saint-Domingue one learned to live with rugged peaks and ridges. "Latibonite" the slaves called the valley, softening the name of the river that meandered in great zigzags out of the mountains separating the Spanish and French parts of the island. It ran through the priceless fields of coffee and cotton, sugar and indigo, out past the salt dunes of La Grande Saline, into the wide Bay of Gonaïves. It was a peaceful river generally, torrential only in times of heavy rain.

Just now it ran quiet and shallow. . .

Pierre closed his book and sat looking at the small eddies among the rocks along the shore. A few yards downstream, some of the younger slave women of the Bérard household were busy washing clothes. With rhythmic energy they beat them upon the rocks until they were clean, then rinsed them in the clear water.

They paced their work with a singsong chant, but the boy was not listening to them.

Nowadays, Pierre came often to the river bank, but not to romp with the other slave children. He had always been the liveliest among them, but lately they had learned to leave him alone when he began to read. It was a mystery to them, this reading—something the white master liked to do.

Pierre was now thirteen years old, tall and strongly built. Several years ago, after her return from France, his grandmother Zénobie had first taken his small hand in her own big one and with a blunt pencil had shown him how to print the letters of his name. From her crude teaching he had quickly learned enough to go far beyond her in the arts of reading and writing.

Later Monsieur Bérard, seeing the boy's real love for books, had given him permission to go into the library at the manor house and read whatever he wished. For hours Pierre would bend over the closely printed pages, spelling out the words laboriously, guessing at meanings, gathering tortuously a knowledge of the world that lay beyond the horizon of a slave. Page after page in worn copybooks had been filled with his attempts to write, awkward at first, but gradually more perfect, and finally even beautiful.

Zénobie always showed Pierre the letters Jean Jacques wrote her from Paris, full of bits of information about the other Bérard children. She would sit down and scrawl an answer in her half-French, half-Creole style. Her grammar and her casual habit of running several words together might well have confounded the French Academy. Such a word as "mother" might appear in many different spellings— sometimes "meure," sometimes "merre." When Pierre would show her the correct spelling in a book, Zénobie would laugh good-naturedly.

"Never mind. He'll know what I mean," she would say.

This particular day Pierre had brought several books with him, but the one that he studied the longest was one he could not even understand—the sermons of the celebrated French preacher, Jean-Baptiste Massillon. Massillon had been a very great preacher in the early days of the reign of Louis XV, and his sermons continued to be much quoted. Often Pierre had heard the Bérards speak of them.

Now he stopped reading and gazed down at the water. Massillon was dead and so was King Louis XV . . . But he wondered what it must have been like to be at the court and hear the great orator speaking. Perhaps then he, Pierre, could have understood everything. Still, he read the sermons over and over again, engraving page after page upon his amazing memory.

A sudden sound startled him, the frightened voice of a young child. He was on his feet in an instant.

"Rosalie?"

He ran to lift a tiny girl, dripping and crying, out of the water. His little sister was never very far away from him, for Ursule, their mother, was busy all day attending to the wants of Madame Bérard. Pierre had looked after her and played with her from the time she was born, and to have allowed this accident to happen to her was a very great disaster.

He carried her up on the shore. He should have watched her more carefully, instead of dreaming about things so far away. Divided between self-blame and fright, he began to scold her for going too far into the water. But she was already miserable enough, her little skirt clinging wetly to her knees, and from the terror that had engulfed her when she slipped on the rocks. So he set her down gently, and playfully pretended he was angry at her for getting him all wet.

She was crying harder and harder. He saw that she had cut her foot a little on one of the sharp rocks. He took a stalk of sugar cane from his pocket and broke off a little piece for her to suck. Then he lifted her again and started up the bank toward the big, rambling manor house.

"Now don't you cry, Rosalie," he was saying. "We'll go and find Gran'mère Zénobie. She'll fix your foot."

It was always to Zénobie the children turned in time of need. All the other slaves at L'Artibonite did the same, for everyone looked up to her as a wise and kindly matriarch.

The Bérards themselves recognized Zénobie's special position. They trusted her completely, even to the remarkable extent of sending their young children abroad to school under her care. With the wisdom of one who had many times assessed life, Zénobie felt no sense of inferiority in a white man's world. The authority of her tribal ancestry rested on her easily and she could command respect as well as love.

Zénobie was, in fact, no longer a slave. In a unique recognition of her service, Monsieur Bérard had made her a freed woman after her second trip to France. But there was no question of her leaving them even then, although legally she could have done so. Everyone expected her to end her days where she had begun them—at Latibonite Plantation.

Pierre and Rosalie found Zénobie in the kitchen. She was ironing one of Madame Bérard's dresses, carefully arranging fold after fold with deft hands.

"What now, children," she called, as she looked up and

saw them crossing the wide veranda toward her.

"We were down by the river, Gran'mère. Rosalie fell in the water," explained Pierre.

"Bring her here, then." Zénobie set her iron back on the stove to keep it hot and perched the little girl on a high stool. She left the room for a moment, then returned with dry clothes for the child. Easing her out of the damp garments, she proceeded to dress the cut.

"I think if you'd tell us a story, she'd forget all about it," Pierre suggested. It was not an altogether unselfish idea. There was nothing Pierre liked so much as to listen to Zénobie's tales.

The foot was soon neatly bandaged in a clean white cloth, and Rosalie's tears subsided as she experimented with hopping about on her uninjured foot, holding the other one up in the air.

Zénobie took up her iron again and tested it with an expert finger. Her hand began to move over the delicately printed muslin.

"Which story then, Pierre?" She was tired and it was a hard thing to say.

Pierre and Rosalie sat down in the doorway looking out over the gardens that stretched from the rear of the house down to the long low wooden sheds where the slaves lived. Nearby Ursule, aided by their elder sister, Marie-Louise, was hanging out long lines of wash.

"How Saint-Domingue became the white man's land—" Pierre prompted.

Zénobie paused thoughtfully, as if she had not told the same story the same way many times before.

"Once there was a man, Christopher Columbus, who sailed three ships across the ocean from Spain. He came looking for a new land. All the men with him were frightened, for they thought they would sail too far, and fall off the edge of the world where it ended.

"But instead they came here. Not very far away from Latibonite they started a little town, Navidad. Then Columbus went back to tell the king of Spain about the beautiful island he had found. But before he left he may have seen our river and many valleys just like this one."

Rosalie's head nodded against Pierre's shoulder. She was almost asleep. But Pierre pictured the whole story as Zénobie talked. It was always this way. The world of L'Artibonite was rich in stories, and Zénobie seemed to know them all, handed down from her own mother Tonette, still living on the plantation. Her lore might have lacked some of the accuracy of history books, but it was far more fascinating.

Years before, famous pirates like Morgan and L'Ollonais had visited Saint-Domingue to hunt wild animals and collect salt from the dunes of La Grande Saline to use in preserving their meat. The nearby island of Tortuga—the Turtle—was the refuge of these plunderers, and there they would return to gloat over their spoils: golden doubloons and pieces of eight stolen from the Spanish caravels. At other times they camped on the western shore of Saint-Domingue. From their method of roasting meat there on open spits—*boucaner*—had come the name of buccaneer.

In Pierre's time, the descendants of these pirates still came to La Grande Saline to barrel salt. The French looked upon them with a wary eye, fearful that their easy way of life might seem too alluring to rebellious slaves. They did not like to bar them altogether, for the income from the selling of salt was too valuable to lose.

Zénobie knew how, in the last fifty years or so, the French

planters had turned much of the jungle land into the huge plantations that sprawled over the valleys, as big as good-sized towns. They built pink and white manor houses, huge homes of many rooms and great windows, surrounded by verandas and terraces where one might sit in the open air, protected from the sun. Close by were planted exquisite formal gardens of magnolia and bougainvillea, poinsettias and frangipani. Marble columns in the porches, elaborate bronze doors, fountains playing gaily over carved statuary, all gave a note of luxury to these homes, the wealthiest places in the New World's richest land.

The whole landscape was dominated by the palm trees that swayed in the slightest breeze. The rest of the land was laid out in immense fields of coffee or cotton plants or thickly-sown sugar cane. There were carriage sheds and large warehouses where bags of coffee and sugar were piled to the ceiling.

The French had also built bridges, irrigation systems, and towns. Their buildings were of the finest stone, hewed from the mountain quarries. They had brought with them from France their own luxurious way of life, and in the tropic wilds of Saint-Domingue they had seen promise of something even greater, a wealth undreamed of even in Parisian drawing rooms.

But looking out over the lush valleys with their gorgeous tropical flowers and exotic trees, they knew that something more was needed before this paradise would yield its riches —the hand of man. And so a royal decree was issued, permitting the planters to bring thirty thousand slaves from Africa.

The solemn pronouncement, given with an appropriate flourish of trumpets and religious solemnity during the regency of Louis XV, stated that the slaves must be saved from the superstitions of the dark continent. In the new colony they would be taught Christianity. It was an ingenious bargain, evidently made in good faith—salvation for the heathen and gold for the coffers of France. To give the decree added importance, it ended with an invocation of the Holy Name of Jesus.

Promulgated as a solemn covenant with God, the decree soon assumed the hollow ring of hypocrisy. Once the slaves were landed in Saint-Domingue, having been uprooted from families and homes in many parts of Africa, they found in their new masters a duplicity that mocked the holy purpose of the plan.

Often the greatest cruelties were inflicted upon them to draw the last bit of profit from their human flesh. And if this were not enough, the Sacraments were often withheld from them because of the embarrassment which might be caused unscrupulous owners if later on they might wish to sell a married slave and break up a family.

Still the French were but a small handful of white men among a sea of African slaves. Nearly every plantation had several hundred slaves, and it was not uncommon to find as many as a thousand belonging to one man. The planters measured their wealth in slaves as much as in land, and the price per slave was then about two hundred and fifty dollars.

The Bérards, unlike so many others, had always kept to the spirit of the decree, teaching their slaves the truths of Faith, permitting them religious marriages, and watching over them with a kindly if paternalistic care. They had even allowed their daughter De Pointe to become Pierre's godmother, thereby showing their solicitude for his spiritual welfare.

Zénobie, of course, did not speak of these things to Pierre, but he had sharp ears. He had overheard many things that were spoken in the slave huts far from any white man's ears.

Sometimes he would beg his grandmother to tell stories from the folklore of their own people. Reluctantly, she would do so. Zénobie was a good Christian and did not believe in the good and evil voodoo spirits that were thought by most of the slaves to inhabit each tree and rock, each river and waterfall. But she was familiar with the ways in which they tried to placate the spirits with *wangas* and other ritualistic bits—chicken feathers, stones and branches tied together just as the *houngan,* or voodoo priest, had directed.

Zénobie was well aware that among the slaves the voodoo superstitions and ritual dances were practiced right along with the Christian observances and liturgy. Not many could distinguish clearly between the two. The slaves with their deep affinity for the supernatural clung tenaciously to their age-old tribal religious customs even as they accepted a new religion.

Officially voodoo was frowned upon by the French but no one dared repress it too rigorously. They could not have done so, anyway. They might pass laws and post guards, but they could never still the drums. Only the slaves knew what the drums were saying.

Up in the hills, hidden from white men's prying eyes, the drums could send strange messages across the whole island in the dead of night, could set it throbbing with weird dancing and wild exultation. And although the whites pretended to scoff at voodoo rites, they had reason to find something terrifying in this mysterious uncensorable language.

CHAPTER 3

THE TROUBLES

When the harvest was ready, the slaves would go through the fields in long files, the sweat pouring from their backs as they cut the cane down to sharp, dry stubble. The swinging of the machetes marked time to their singing; the sugar harvests, one after another, seemed to mark time in their lives.

For Pierre the childhood years were passing. He had come to the legal age for work. Others at this time, sent to toil in pickaninny gangs, learned with brutal suddenness what it really meant to be a slave. But Pierre was more fortunate. He had become a household servant, trained to domestic duties and attendance upon members of a gentle family.

At L'Artibonite many things were changing. Jean Jacques Bérard had returned at last from Paris, his studies finished, ready to take up the direction of plantation affairs. For a long time the elder Bérards had dreamed of leaving L'Artibonite to his management and going back to their beloved France to live. Now they were about to realize that dream, for they felt that Jean had not only grown up, he was competent. They could have confidence in him. He spoke well on many subjects. He knew all the talk of Paris, the great debates over Voltaire, Rousseau, and Diderot. He told of fierce verbal battles going on over current political events. But when he mentioned *Les Amis des Noirs,* the discussion always grew very serious, for this new society, founded by Brisson de Warville, onetime visitor to the American colonies and later leader of the Gironde, was promoting the cause of the men of color in Saint-Domingue, bringing with it considerable bitterness and even violence.

Pierre probably knew little of the controversy raging between the men of color and the colonial government. But he must have been aware of the growing ill feeling on the island.

The trouble centered chiefly around the demands of the *gens de couleur* for a voice in the Saint-Domingue government. These people, the offspring of many mixed unions, had widely varying percentages of black and white blood. So many combinations existed that a writer of the time, Moreau de Saint Méry, meticulously defined sixty-four blood differences, each with its own name — *sang mêlé, mulatto, griffe, quateron, mustif.* Indeed, skin color was society's dominant preoccupation.

Many of the plantation owners had endowed their black mistresses and children with lands and freedom, even setting them up with their own slaves. Some of the *gens de couleur* imitated the wealthy whites in sending their children abroad to be educated. Here the difficulties began, for by the laws of France the inhabitants of Saint-Domingue were entitled to all the privileges of French citizens. In Paris they learned to enjoy these privileges. But when they returned home it was a different story.

The planters were afraid of the growing influence of the men of color, and persistently ignored the ancient laws of the mother country regarding equality. It was easy for them to do so because they had their own assemblies at Cap Français and Saint Marc, where subservient government officials could be induced to pass over the rights of those of mixed blood. The planters, contributing immense sums of money to the royal treasury through taxes, were determined that their opponents should have no voice in political affairs.

They tried to subdue the men of color by foolish laws born of fear. They forbade them to practice medicine, for they thought that anyone possessing slave blood had an instinctive knowledge of poisoning; nor could they become priests, for it was unthinkable that one with slave blood should hear the confession of a white man. Law, pharmacy, school teaching, public office, all were closed to them, and the art of the goldsmith was also forbidden, since it offered a possibility of great wealth. Even the clothing of the *gens de couleur* was dictated by law, for the planters were jealous of their own sartorial splendor. Something like madness was sweeping over the island, gripping everyone with ominous terror or seething resentment.

Not far from L'Artibonite itself stood a grim reminder of violence in other days. Crête à Pierrot, the black mountain fortress, now covered with dense tangled jungle growth, had been the last refuge of the planters in an earlier slave revolt. Now they thought of it again. Should the terror strike, one could always hide there, safe behind the guns, until the rebels subsided.

The elder Bérards, looking out for the last time over their

fields and gardens, may have felt some sense of foreboding, a shadow passing momentarily across a smiling scene. This time they boarded the ship for France with misgivings. But after all, Jean, younger and more confident, might be better able to face the troubled future than they. Besides they had with them the faithful Zénobie, their staunch consoler, whom they had asked to accompany them home. One more strenuous sea voyage, the old woman thought, and then she would lead a quiet life back in the valley of L'Artibonite among her own people.

If young Jean shared his parents' premonitions, he saw at least no immediate cause for worry. The sun shone at Saint Marc with a brightness remembered from his boyhood, such as he had never seen elsewhere in his travels. He was busy with all the details of running a big plantation. It was like owning a village of one's own.

Like his father, Jean was reasonable and fair, inclined to the conservative view. Above all, he was Christian in his attitude toward the slaves and the men of color. He continually urged an understanding, but the other planters were not sympathetic to his stand. Some of them were no longer so cordial when he stopped to exchange greetings with them after Sunday Mass in Saint Marc.

They openly expressed their disapproval of his kindly attitude toward his slaves. Permitting them sacramental marriage as he did was strictly against the planters' code, for such a practice could cause great inconvenience. Besides, to give a slave a sense of dignity was to permit the reins of power to slip a little from the white man's hand.

Religion might lead a slave to discover that he too had been created by Almighty God for love.

But Jean Bérard did not intend to change his opinions.

His plantation continued to prosper, and there was his approaching wedding to turn his mind from the turbulent political affairs of the Colony.

Pierre and Rosalie and all the other slaves were busied for weeks with the preparations. The manor house was decorated with flowers and palms and the guests came from all around the valley to help celebrate the day.

Of the friends and neighbors who came many were well known to Pierre. Among them were the three daughters of Louis Bossard and his wife Anne, wealthy plantation owners in neighboring Dondon in the towering Marmalade Mountains to the north. Marie Anne was married to General Dessource of the Saint Marc regiment while Marie Elisabeth was the wife of Monsieur Roudanès. Adeline, the third sister, was single. From childhood, the three girls had been nursed by Pierre's aunt, Marie Bouquement, and they greeted him with affectionate kindliness on their arrival.

Out on the lawn, protected by gay sunshades of many colors, a huge barbecue was set up among banks of flowers. Here the cooks presided anxiously over the meats roasting on spits, succulent yams and artichokes, and that special French delicacy—truffles—island-grown. Champagne brought from France was plentiful. Even the slaves had a holiday from the field work, and *tafia,* their favorite drink, a raw rum made from sugar cane. And there was music. The ever-present tambours beating out the dance rhythms, with melodies played on flutes and violins, and the lively staccato of the *maracas.*

Pierre loved parties. Music and dancing were his heart. But his eyes were keen. Amid all the merriment and confusion he noticed especially how tired the young bride looked. Many years later, he was to describe her as she appeared that day.

"I remember her when the bridal took place. She was very pale; and her health was always delicate, but she looked so lovely and we were all so happy! And Rosalie and I never tired of gathering flowers for her."

"Gathering flowers for her" —that was to be the theme for the year to come. Jean Bérard made Pierre and Rosalie personal attendants upon their new mistress. They were not only to wait upon her, but to make her smile often, for they were naturally gay. Sometimes the hours passed too slowly for the women of the manor. They had little to do, and social life was very limited. The sun which made the country so fruitful was not always kind to those who sat in the great lonely houses and thought of France, so far away. It would beat down mercilessly, and at times the air inland, in the valley, grew very still as though it would never stir again. Then Pierre with his violin, his mimicry, his rhythmic feet, his good humor, could be a blessed relief.

It seemed, that first year, that even with all the mounting tensions in the plantations around them, life at L'Artibonite could still be peaceful and pleasant. Then the sadness came.

Young Madame Bérard became very ill with tuberculosis. Paler and weaker than ever, she breathed with difficulty the heavy air. The doctor thought a change of climate might help her, and suggested a trip to some place nearer the sea.

Pierre and Rosalie accompanied her to Port-au-Prince, the principal city of Saint-Domingue's southern peninsula. Along the way Pierre tried to keep everyone in good spirits, but it was a somber party that traveled the long dusty road winding precariously between the mountains and the coast. They carried her as gently as possible across the narrow mountain torrents, many without even the rudest of bridges, in their bumping hardwheeled carriage. In the little town of Mont Roui they paused for a while so that she might rest, and then continued on their way to Port-au-Prince.

But it was a wasted journey. Their young mistress was never to return to her home. Nothing could bring her back to health and in one short month she died. She was only twenty-one.

Pierre and Rosalie returned sadly to L'Artibonite. This close acquaintance with death touched the young slaves deeply, and Pierre, mysteriously thoughtful beneath his outward gaiety, spoke of it often in his later life.

"I can see her as she lay upon the couch, panting for air —all so beautiful outside and in. Then Rosalie and I would stand at opposite corners of the room and pull the strings of a magnificent fan of peacock feathers, swaying it to and fro, and we would laugh and be so gay, that she would smile too. But she never grew stronger; she grew weaker."

CHAPTER 4

THE OTHER TOUSSAINT

During the years Pierre had spent puzzling over Monsieur Bérard's books, there was another slave in Saint-Domingue who was similarly occupied. This was the man who was to make the name Toussaint known the world over, so that today the word instantly calls up the image of a dank dungeon, a line from a Wordsworth sonnet, a tiny cell in the Jura Mountains where, in 1803, Toussaint L'Ouverture, sometimes called "The First of the Blacks," was to die of cold, starvation and Napoleon's vengeance.

But while Pierre was growing up at L'Artibonite, L'Ouverture was working with the other slaves at Breda, the beautiful estate owned by the Comte de Noé about three miles from the elegant capital of Cap Français. It lay across the Black Mountains from the Bérard plantation, on the island's northern plain.

Pierre's ancestry is buried deep in Congo mystery, but we know that the other Toussaint was the son of an African king, distinguished even in slavery by royal blood. A sickly and melancholy boy, he had learned reading, writing, and numbers from his godfather, an old black worker at the hospital of the Fathers of Charity in Cap Français.

Monsieur Libertat, the "factor" of Breda, had recognized the young slave as a born leader, and an astute judge of men and conditions. He had made L'Ouverture steward of the plantation, a responsibility no slave had held before.

It is strange how much the two Toussaints had in common. Two slaves with the same name, born within the same quarter century on the same island. They both had kindly masters, and what was more unusual, masters who actually encouraged them to read and learn. After all, it might have been uncomfortable for a master to own a slave who knew too much! Led on by their individual ambitions, both had acquired knowledge quite uncommon to persons in their circumstances.

Striking as were their likenesses, their differences were even more so. In 1758, when Toussaint L'Ouverture was fifteen years old, he happened to be in Cap Français one terrible January afternoon when the notorious runaway slave Macandal was burned to death in the Place Royale. Probably he made little or no comment on what he had seen. He was never one to let others share his thoughts, and this was to be one of the sources of his mysterious power later on. But the sight of that pyre must have kindled another fire in the boy, one that burned bitterly in secret for a long time before it broke out and seared the whole of Saint-Domingue. It set L'Ouverture upon his life's course, from which he was, with dogged perseverance, never to vary for an instant for the rest of his career.

Thus while Pierre had read with admiration the sermons

of Massillon and Bossuet, the other Toussaint had avidly devoured the military exploits of Alexander the Great and Julius Caesar. Pierre had committed to memory many passages from the spiritual writers. L'Ouverture took care to remember secrets of battlefield strategy as described in the writings of experts. Pierre reflected on the Beatitudes — "Blessed are the peacemakers"; L'Ouverture, though he knew the Bible well, meditated on the vocation to which he felt himself divinely appointed—the annihilation of those who had made slaves of his people. And he proceeded on his course so quietly, so stealthily, that those around him never suspected that he bore the slightest discontent, or that he dreamed of any life other than driving the elegant coach of Monsieur Libertat, and making Breda the wealthiest plantation in all the country around Cap Français. In Pierre there was never any deception. He never saw an enemy in any man, and only charity mitigated his candor.

The moment was to come when the obscure slave of Breda would see his mysterious conviction of his calling coincide with a political crisis that would shake France and her Caribbean colony in an ague of violence. Then Toussaint L'Ouverture would be ready to climb down from his coachman's seat and take over the leadership of the masses of rebel slaves on the island. He would step fully prepared into a struggle between the white and the *gens de couleur,* seizing an opportune hour to strike for the freedom of the slaves.

Pierre, on the other hand, was never known to take the side of violence in any dispute. In fact, he never took part in disputes at all. He too had seen at first hand the ignominy of oppression. Like L'Ouverture, his superior mind and sensitive nature must have been shocked often by the injustices he saw. But one of the strange things about Pierre was his lack of resentment. He always looked upon other men, not as partisans of creed or color, but as sons of his own Father in Heaven.

In those years of growing conflict Pierre could see the tension all around him in the valley. The planters secretly harbored an awful fear of those they had so greatly mistreated. The slaves themselves were saved from utter despair by their own peculiarly resilient temperament. If the day was filled with grueling work in the burning fields, the night brought release—song and the wild joy of the dancing.

Mungo Park, the famed African traveler, wrote: "Every evening, when the sun goes down, all Africa is alive with dance and song. The sound of music, rude though it be, stirs the leaves of the palm trees from the marts of Ophir to the coast of Congo." He might have been describing the slave world of Saint-Domingue.

When evening fell, brutal punishments were forgotten, burnings and brandings and sadistic tortures were cast away like evil spirits. Even after the relentless hours of labor, the hopeless round of toil and more toil, the slaves could dance. The drummers had their haunts up in the hills, and the white men would lie restless in their hand-carved beds, listening to the voodoo rhythms, feeling themselves surrounded, held captive by those they persecuted. Sometimes—it was only an illusion—the drums seemed to be drawing nearer, nearer, and the silent feet of wild dancers drew tight circles around the sleepless masters, enclosing them in shadowy chains.

Jean Bérard was among the few who could rest with a clear conscience, for he had always tried to follow the way of peace and justice. But even he could finally see that violence was bound to come. As he had no desire either to participate in the fight or to jeopardize his own wealth and well-being, he began to think out a plan. Why not go away for a while, leave the island until the inevitable storm had passed and calm had come again?

France would have been the logical refuge. All the rest of the Bérard family were now living there. But affairs in that country were hardly favorable to aristocrats just then. It seemed wiser to look toward the North American continent. The colonies had just successfully concluded their war for independence against Britain, and were settling down to their own course as an infant nation. Jean Bérard had business connections in New York, and he had no difficulty in arranging for a visit there.

The young master of L'Artibonite had married again, this time bringing to the plantation the young Marie Elisabeth Roudanès, lately a widow. A daughter of the Bossard family, she had long been on terms of intimacy with the Bérards. Like Jean she was wealthy in her own right, for both her father and mother had bequeathed riches to her. Her mother had been a member of the Fleury family, long-time residents of Dondon, a parish lying between L'Artibonite and Cap Français. The Fleurys were one of the seven or eight original families to settle in that place. Dondon had received many of the Acadians expelled from Canada, and the latter had married with the earlier colonists, so it is possible that the new Madame Bérard had Acadian blood in her veins.

When Jean Bérard proposed the idea of a voyage to the States, it was welcomed by his wife. Her two sisters, Marie Anne Dessource and Adeline Bossard, also wanted to go along. Of course, their nurse Marie Bouquement must come too. Monsieur Bérard decided to take Pierre and Rosalie as well as two other slaves, for their help would be needed in setting up a temporary household abroad.

Once the decision was made, Jean Bérard and his wife did not long delay their departure. From Saint Marc one could get passage on any one of the many ships trading with the New World metropolis. They sailed sometime in 1787, their vessel taking the famous course up through the Windward Passage, calling in briefly at the big harbor of Cap Français, filled with vessels from all over the world, before heading into the powerful Gulf Stream that would carry them toward New York.

The stop at Cap Français was probably the closest the two Toussaints ever came to meeting. Pierre was twenty-one then, an age for courage and the spirit of adventure. Still, he had glimpsed with horror the rising violence on the island—terrors that would make the French Revolution seem almost civilized—and he must have felt the gravity of the situation that forced his master to take refuge in a strange land.

Though they all believed the parting to be for only a short time, Pierre was never again to see Ursule, his mother, or Zénobie, or any of the other members of his own family. As the boat passed the rocky promontory that guards the harbor of Cap Français from the sea, he was leaving behind forever the people and places of his childhood.

CHAPTER 5

FIRST DAYS IN NEW YORK

In 1787 the maternal arms of New York harbor were already reaching out hospitably to welcome the refugee. Unmistakably majestic and impressive was the approach to the Manhattan of those days. It was a small but energetic city, just now rising resolutely from the destruction wrought by the War of Independence, and showing already that penchant for commerce that was to distinguish it before the world.

The ship carrying the Bérards arrived under a fresh breeze and a sky of rare blue.

"See, Pierre, so many ships, all at once!" His sister Rosalie pointed excitedly as she and the others of the party crowded the ship's rails for the first look at their destination. They had been used to watching the movements in the bustling harbor of Saint Marc, but here were more ships than they had ever seen, all bearing strange cargoes and the flags of far-off lands.

Jean Bérard held his wife's arm protectively. His thoughts were mostly on the details of the arrival, for he was a very practical man. He could not help being a bit worried. Would the house that had been leased for them be satisfactory? After all, he had not seen it. Would the furnishings make the women of the household feel happy and at home? How would he find sound investments for the money he had brought along to support them during their stay? And always in the back of his mind was L'Artibonite and the troubles that overshadowed it. How would it all turn out? Questions kept flying through his mind as the ship nosed cautiously toward her pier at the foot of Wall Street.

Adeline Bossard was busy saying good-by to shipboard acquaintances. Marie Anne, the third sister, was hurriedly finishing her letter to her husband, General Dessource, assuring him of their safe arrival, for the ship's captain had promised to deliver the letter in person upon his return to Saint-Domingue. The tedious three-week passage had been lightened by the companionship of other French-speaking passengers. Now when they stepped off the ship they would enter a new world, completely strange, even in its language. They had enjoyed wealth and popularity at home. Here? Well at least it was only for a little while!

Rosalie, youngest of the slaves, was jumping up and down pointing out this and that, exclaiming over everything. Now the ships. Now the people. And then the trees gracefully lining the Battery—so different from the palms of Saint-Domingue.

But her brother Pierre had scarcely time to notice the scenery. He was so busy running around seeing to the baggage and trying not to forget anything at the last minute. The three ladies had brought enough luggage for many years, it seemed to him. Trunk after trunk packed with frilled gowns and exquisite accessories. And hats! It was the hats that gave Pierre the most trouble, for they were simply unpackable. Not a ribbon must be creased, not a velvet petal crumpled. He had tried them this way and that, all the way up the harbor, but there was always a net trailing or a feather sticking up when he attempted to put on the lid. It needed patience. At last he had everything ready. He was standing by the bags waiting for Monsieur Bérard to arrange for them to disembark.

As the boat docked near the foot of Wall Street the whole wharfside was busy, filled with merchants and merchants' helpers, eager to bid on whatever cargo the ship might bear.

In the midst of the confusion, a young man came toward the hesitating Bérard party, breaking through the crowd of passengers and barterers.

"Oh, here you are, Jean," he greeted them in the familiar accents of the island they had left. "We were afraid you might not have been able to get away in time."

The words "in time," rang strangely in Jean's mind. A sort of blackness seemed to descend with them, but it passed quickly into delight and relief at seeing his friend. He had traveled a good deal, but even so it was bewildering to come into a strange country without knowing its language, and he was glad to have immediate help. This was the same friend who had made arrangements for leasing the house they were to occupy. And he had very thoughtfully brought along a carriage to take them there.

"You'll see to the luggage then, Pierre." Jean turned to his slave. "Have you enough money for the porter?"

"Yes, Monsieur, but there will be the customs first, I understand," replied Pierre.

"That shouldn't take long. We'll go on ahead in the carriage."

Jean handed Pierre a slip of paper with the street and number. Rosalie and her aunt, Marie Bouquemont, were picking up the handbags and a few personal belongings as they helped Madame Bérard and her sisters toward the carriage.

Pierre followed the burly porter and his awkward wheelbarrow through the crowded street. Away from the wharf and up The Broadway. They could not travel very fast. Pierre tried to take in everything they passed. The noisy barrow bumped along the uneven cobblestones without a care in the world for the Bossard ladies' hats or the other delicate objects it was carrying.

All around him the air resounded with the noise of commerce, the peculiar haste that pervades the exchange of money and goods. How different the buildings looked, from those of Pierre's native island—all so straight and proper, almost frowning down at him with their prim gables. There was nothing bright or fanciful like the tropical colors, the artful architecture of Saint-Domingue. Some of the buildings still bore the scars of the great fire of the previous year. The gutted remains stood like ghost figures against the clear sky.

Now the people became fewer, the streets more countrylike, and the houses were farther and farther apart. Pierre saw instantly that the heart of the city was the waterfront, the source of its revenue. By the time they passed Saint Paul's Church on The Broadway, even the cobblestones had ended. It was only the deep ruts in the dirt road that jolted the barrow and brought angry ejaculations from the porter. Pierre was just as happy that he could not understand.

He felt more at home now as he grew used to walking on land again. Besides, they had come into green fields, trees

and country lanes. To the left he could look down Chatham
Street toward The Bowery and its farms and little Dutch
houses. He was glad they would not be living too close to the
docks. Soon they were at Reade Street, their destination.

Even as the three Bossard sisters were lifting their
gorgeous dresses from their wrappings in the trunks, they
were busy planning their first party—whom to invite, what
refreshments to serve. They already knew a few people among
the French colony, and they expected to meet more very soon.
They hoped to make their home gay, hospitable, entertaining.
Jean Bérard encouraged their frivolous planning. He wanted
them, so far as possible, to live as they had always lived,
during this short exile.

One day he called Pierre to him.

"I have a new trade for you," he said, "something you've
never done before."

Pierre was puzzled, but he answered quickly.

"Whatever you wish, Monsieur."

"I've arranged for you to learn hairdressing," Jean Bérard
explained. "A Mr. Merchant who has a shop here has
promised to take you as an apprentice. He will teach you all
he knows of the coiffeur's art."

"Very well, Monsieur," replied Pierre, "but do you think
I'll be able to learn?" He tried to form a picture of himself,
scissors in hand.

"Oh, of course you will, Pierre. No fear about that. You're
very quick. You'll be able to dress the hair of Mademoiselle
Adeline, and Madame Dessource, as well as of Madame
Bérard. It will be nice for them to have their own coiffeur right
here in the house, and besides—" he spoke half-seriously,
"you know, Pierre, you're the only man of this household,

besides myself, and it's always good to know a trade."

Pierre did not question his new assignment. In fact, he found he really liked the work, and from the very beginning Mr. Merchant knew he had a gifted pupil. Pierre's fingers certainly had a deftness that was not merely acquired. He worked hard mastering the hair styles that were in fashion —styles that now seem to us so massive and ludicrous. In those days a really fashionable lady might spend as much as a thousand dollars a year to have her hair dressed daily by a coiffeur who called at her home before the social activities began.

Pierre began by learning to cut children's hair. Soon he was working on some of Mr. Merchant's grown-up customers. Some of them asked especially to have Pierre, for he was courteous as well as clever.

New York was the capital of the thirteen colonies. On July 26, 1788, the state would ratify the Constitution helping to make the country into a more complete unity. In 1789, two years after Pierre's arrival, the city witnessed the triumphal inauguration of Washington as first President of the United States. Thereafter New Yorkers were often to see the President leaving his home at No. 3 Cherry Street for his daily walk around the Battery, wearing his black velvet suit, his dress sword at his side, and upon his brow the heavy lines of care.

Far to the north of the city in a suburb called Greenwich Village, Abigail Adams, the wife of the Vice- President, was busy regaling her correspondents with tales of the heavy requirements of social life. In the New York of that day this called more for endurance than for the evanescent qualities of wit or charm. Indeed it was almost as monumental and just about as spontaneous as the tiered curls atop every fashionable female head. In the afternoons the stately procession of coaches might be seen bearing the finely gowned and coiffed ladies of leading families out along Greenwich Street to pay a state visit or to attend a weekly "at home." Mrs. John Jay, Mrs. George Washington, General Knox's wife—all had their fixed days for guests. But Mrs. Adams' levees, in her big house in the Village, were perhaps the most popular.

"I have returned more than sixty visits," she wrote, "all of them in 3 or 4 afternoons excepting the President's, have drank tea only at two other places and dined but once out, since I arrived."

Again: "I could give an account of visiting and receiving visits, but in that there is so little variety that one letter might contain the whole history. For instance on Monday evenings, Mrs. Adams receives company. That is her rooms are lighted and put in order. Servants and Gentlemen and Ladies, as many as inclination, curiosity or Fashion tempts, come out to make their Bow and Curtzy, take Coffee and Tea, chat an half hour, or longer, and then return to town again."

The number of guests might vary from a few to seven hundred, for these receptions in the homes were the main events of social life. The John Street Theater was the only one in New York, and other outside amusements were very few.

On the night of Washington's inauguration, April 30, 1789, the Spanish minister, Don Diego de Gardoqui, had given a memorable party at his residence at No. 1, The Broadway. The guests were astonished at the magnificence of the affair, which took place in a setting of colored lights, with a background of moving pictures etched in glass, depicting scenes described by Mrs. Adams as a veritable "fairy land."

Because of the help the French King Louis XVI had given the Colonies, a feeling of warm good will existed between the Americans and the French. The Bérards found it easy to make new friends.

Pierre liked parties as much as anyone. Gaiety was one of his gifts, and everyone expected him to liven things up when the Bérards were entertaining.

"I remember Toussaint among the slaves," an acquaintance of those happy days recalled, "dressed in a red jacket, full of spirits, and very fond of dancing and music, and always devoted to his mistress who was young, gay and planning future enjoyment."

"Come now, Pierre, play something for us," the guests would beg. And Pierre would set down his serving tray and take up his violin. His little gold earrings would glitter brightly in the lamplight while he smilingly called from the strings some lively tune.

But Jean Bérard could not enter fully into the spirit of his wife's quest for amusement. Always he seemed preoccupied. Pierre knew he worried greatly over affairs back home, for his master haunted the wharves, learning from incoming ships the latest word of the violence brooding over L'Artibonite. He began seriously to wonder whether they would ever be reunited in that peaceful valley again.

So far Jean had no immediate financial worries, for the money he had brought with him seemed safely invested and would support them awhile longer. But from the scant news by letter and the ominous talk in the merchant offices downtown there was little hope of their returning to Saint-Domingue for some time. And when they did go—what would they find? Did their home still stand? He did not even know.

Jean did not say much about these things which disturbed him so deeply. Perhaps he did not want to worry Marie. When he could no longer bear the uncertainty he made up his mind to go back to Saint Marc alone. He wanted to see for himself what was happening in Saint-Domingue, and to salvage what he could from the family estate. He made his preparations, and in 1789 boarded a ship for the island, followed by the prayers of the household for his safe voyage.

Chapter 6

The Blow of Fortune

In May 1789 Washington had been in office less than a month. New York was still basking in the festive glow of the inauguration when suddenly word came from Paris that the States-General, the French Parliament, had been summoned for the first time in one hundred and fifty years. The royal authority was in question.

To Saint-Domingue, thousands and thousands of ocean miles from Paris, the news was a torch to turn the smoldering discontent of all factions into a raging fire. By this time each side had its own bitter grievance. The planters wanted more freedom from the arbitrary rule of the French court. The freedmen, encouraged by the success of the American Revolution, were pressing their demands through their Paris spokesmen, *Les Amis des Noirs.* And far from the conference tables, in canebrake and tumble-down huts and hilly refuges, throbbed the sore resentment of seven hundred thousand slaves!

Two tense months passed. Then came the fall of the Bastille and the end of the *ancien régime.* The National Assembly in Paris, after a debate, decided to support the claims of the men of color. Their leaders, the mulattos Ogé and Chavannes, returned triumphant to Saint-Domingue to demand their political rights from the island government.

But the planters had no intention of giving in, and angrily refused the freedmen's demands, despite the Assembly's ruling. Violence broke out immediately, but the *gens de couleur* were of course unable to make a strong stand against the powerful planters and were quickly beaten down with brutal savagery. Ogé and Chavannes and the other leaders were put to death in the public square of Cap Français, their bodies broken on the wheel or hanged from scaffolds.

It was in this year that Jean Bérard returned to the island. He arrived in the midst of tumult. In New York, his wife waited and worried. She would look up anxiously each evening as Pierre came in from his daily visit to the wharves for news from the trading ships. He knew her questions before she spoke. But the tales told by French refugees from Saint-Domingue only filled her with dismay.

At last a letter came from Jean.

"Good news today, Madame." Pierre smiled cheerfully as he handed his mistress the envelope. He hoped the letter would relieve her worries.

As he turned to go out of the room Madame Bérard motioned to him to stay.

"Wait a moment, Pierre. Maybe there's a message for you in the letter." Madame Bérard was a fearful person and having Pierre there made it easier to open the envelope.

Things were not going well. Surrounded by strife and macabre outbreaks of violence, Jean wrote in despair that there was no hope at all for peace. Saint-Domingue was in an uproar, and over it hung the greatest threat of all—the fear that the slaves too were ready to revolt!

"Do not entertain any thoughts of returning home in the immediate future," he said. "As to our property, my dear Marie, I fear that we will be unable to control its destiny. We must wait to see whether it will be spared from destruction."

Marie read the letter aloud. She could hardly believe what Jean's words told her. He was usually so capable and confident. Now he seemed to expect only the worst. Pierre, however, realized only too well the significance of his master's concern. There was, as Jean had said, nothing to do but wait and pray.

"Monsieur Bérard will find some way out, Madame," he comforted her. He must try to keep up her courage. She was very young, and as inexperienced as a child in the hard ways of life. "Please do not be so concerned. We can manage things here until things take a better turn and Monsieur Bérard is back here again. God will help us."

"I pray he will, Pierre," answered Marie sadly. "Do you think Father O'Brien would remember Jean at Mass tomorrow?"

"I'm certain of it, Madame. I'll go and speak to him at once."

On the way out he stopped downstairs in the kitchen. A cup of tea, brought upstairs to her room, might do Madame good, he told Rosalie.

As he walked down Church Street on the way to the pastor's house, he was thinking of ways to distract his mistress in the days ahead. She must not be left to brood too much, for she had a somewhat melancholy nature. He would try to turn her mind toward the happy day of her husband's return.

He turned slowly into Barclay Street, deep in thought. Before going to speak to Father O'Brien, he stopped for a few moments in St. Peter's Church. It was a habit he had. . .

From that day on they made many plans for Monsieur Bérard's homecoming—even though they did not know when it would be. Madame Bérard was always happy when planning a party or some other entertainment, and Pierre encouraged this to keep her occupied. Despite his propensity to deep seriousness he could change in a moment to a mood of wonderful gaiety, and if he ever thought of the few terrible scenes of violence he had witnessed back in Saint Domingue he did not speak of them. Instead, he devoted himself enthusiastically to planning a grand welcome for the master's return.

He kept up his daily visits to the Wall Street docks, looking for letters, for some word to keep up Madame Bérard's spirits. He listened to the talk of those coming off the West Indies vessels.

A flood of refugees was pouring into New York. In Paris the king had been removed from power, though not yet executed. The Reign of Terror had still to come. The full meaning of the French Revolution was dawning slowly in the minds of those rich merchants and people of nobility who now frantically sought haven in New York and other American cities. The people of the States were largely on the side of the Revolution, for they saw in it another victory for self-government, similar to their own.

One day a ship's captain handed Pierre another letter for his mistress. He saw that it was not addressed in Monsieur Bérard's familiar and precise hand, and it was with grave premonitions that he came back to Reade Street and found

Madame Bérard. She was working on her embroidery—one of the set of petit point chair covers she hoped to finish before Jean came back, the design a gorgeous bird with feathers of many colors.

Her pale face grew even whiter as she saw the strange handwriting on the letter Pierre carried, and her hand shook as she tried to settle her needle in the heavy canvas.

"Open it, Pierre," she said. "You read it."

He unfolded the single sheet. It was only a short note announcing that Jean Jacques Bérard had suddenly died of pleurisy in Saint-Domingue!

Marie Bérard's embroidery slipped to the floor, and her bird of paradise in his brilliant plumage lay crumpled on the carpet. Pierre went quickly to call her sisters.

On the far-off island where Jean Bérard's body rested, a weird conclave had been called. On a stormy night in August, 1791, the braver spirits among the slaves met in a deep forest to plot a rebellion!

Boukman, a runaway slave who had sworn vengeance against the white man, spoke to them in words burning with passion. While lightning flashed in the night sky and thunder rolled portentously overhead, he stood before them in a red ceremonial robe performing the ritualistic voodoo sacrifice. We are told that in that ominous hour a young girl drank a death potion and fell at the feet of the worshippers, offering herself as a victim to the spirits that they might come to the aid of her people in their fight for freedom.

Drawing himself up with bizarre dignity, Boukman harangued his half-maddened listeners:

"Good God, who makes the sun to light us from on high, who raises up the sea and makes the storm to thunder—

Good God who watches over all, hidden in a cloud, protect and save us from what the white men do to us. Good God, the white men do crimes, but we do not. Good God, give us vengeance, guide our arms, give us help. Negroes, show the image of the Good God to the white men, that we thirst not. Good God, grant us that freedom which speaks to all men."

That night the awful vengeance broke over all the northern plain, with burnings, lootings, and massacres that left hardly a white man, woman, or child living around Cap Français. Beautiful chateaux went up in flames, one after another, and the air reeked of charred sugar and charred flesh.

Toussaint L'Ouverture, Dessalines, and Henri Christophe soon rallied the slaves and were leading them in ruthless destruction down from the mountains across the whole island. In Saint-Domingue, the white man's day was done.

In the grief-stricken Bérard household in New York, Pierre went quietly about the business of shouldering all cares. In his native land, slaves were abandoning their masters, in order to destroy them. But Jean Bérard, as he lay dying, could have thanked God that at least he had left a slave like Pierre to watch over his family.

CHAPTER 7

REFUGEES IN NEW YORK

Madame Bérard lifted the delicate gold brooch from her jewel box and looked at it lovingly. She remembered so well the day she had first seen it. It was her birthday, and her father Louis Bossard had greeted her with the little satin box as soon as she came downstairs. She had opened it, with joyous exclamations, the whole family crowding around her, their waiting breakfast forgotten. At this memory tears started in her eyes, but she shook her head impatiently to drive them away. No time for that now. She must face the facts.

Hurriedly she thrust the brooch in the velvet bag with all the other pieces—rings, bracelets, necklaces. Quickly wrapping them together, she tied the package with a piece of red ribbon. Red for courage.

A knock at the door, and Pierre came in.

"You called me, Madame?"

"Yes," she said, trying to steady her voice. "I want you to

do something for me, Pierre. Take this package. It is jewelry. Do you think you could sell it for me?"

"Sell it, Madame!" Pierre was plainly shocked. "But —"

"Yes. That's what I said." She spoke almost sharply in her embarrassment. "They should be worth at least—forty dollars." She finished up lamely. How could she ever hide anything from Pierre? He would have to know sooner or later.

She needed the money so badly. It had been humiliating enough this afternoon when the gentleman had called to ask for payment of a personal debt of Jean's. But to have to put him off because she did not have it! Marie Bérard did not feel equal to such a situation. She had never faced one like it before. Of course the man had meant to cause her no anxiety. He simply assumed, as did everyone else, that the wealthy Jean Bérard had left his young wife very well off indeed.

Pierre still stood before her, puzzled.

"Do you remember, Pierre, the money Monsieur Bérard invested in business when we first came here to New York?"

Of course Pierre remembered, very well. It was to have been their only means of support.

She continued bravely:

"It's gone. Lost, I mean. The firm has failed."

Instantly Pierre's quick mind grasped the meaning of this news. So they were penniless! Poor Madame! First she had lost her husband, and now all her money. He took the little package and went away.

Several days later he was back again, bringing her the bag of jewelry still unopened. And in another package, forty dollars.

Marie was shocked to find Pierre with so much money at hand.

"Where did you get this, Pierre?"

"It's part of my savings, Madame," he answered. "I've had it for a long time." As a slave he was allowed to have a certain amount of money of his own and often received gifts on special occasions from his owner.

Then the tears did come to Marie Bérard's eyes—tears she had been fighting to keep back for days. His kindness unnerved her. But, to take money from one's slave! Still, what else could she do?

"Take it, Madame," Pierre urged.

"I'll pay it back to you soon, Pierre. You know our estates on the island will soon be settled, and then—you'll have this back, and more!"

A few days later he brought her another bill, this one already marked "Paid."

To the question he saw unspoken in her eyes, he replied quietly:

"Mr. Merchant is very good to me. He lets me have some of the customers for myself—the ones that are not so fashionable. Besides, I still have all the money you have given me—my New Year's presents."

So now Pierre was earning money. It was on his salary as a hairdresser that Madame Bérard and the rest of the household would have to get along. Pierre considered carefully how to manage it on his slender income. He was familiar with most of the household expenses, more so, probably, than his mistress. Above all, she must be spared the pain of begging from her slave. He would turn over his earnings to her regularly, keeping as little as possible for his own needs.

Madame Bérard, hardly out of her teens, was now in complete charge of a large household, and with no financial resources—except Pierre's aid. Her two sisters, and their slaves too, depended on her for support.

She cried bitterly over her misfortunes. Pierre told later how trying those days had been.

"It was a sad period for my poor mistress, but she believed —we all believed—that she could recover her property in the West Indies. She was rich in her own right, as well as her husband's, and we said, 'O, Madame! You will have enough!'"

And she did. But not, as she had expected, the gold of the Indies. It was, instead, the hard-earned money of a conscientious slave.

Now began the years when Pierre would spend every minute he could spare from his work at his mistress' side. For time, though it softened the shock of her widowhood, never assuaged her sorrow. Formerly so gay, so fond of good times, the young girl had now become virtually a recluse, melancholy and withdrawn. She brooded over the fact that she had not been able to be with her husband during his last hours. She no longer took an interest in parties or friends. Pierre alone could really console her, for her sisters were as distraught as she. Day followed day, with only Pierre's firm faith and quiet courage to sustain them.

They lived on hope. Like all the other exiles from Saint-Domingue they expected the French government eventually to win back their lands and estates for them. They could not believe that a mob of slaves with the most primitive weapons could hold off for long the power of the organized military.

But it was an empty dream for them and for all the destitute or near-destitute planters seeking refuge on American soil. In the Southern States, developments in Saint-Domingue were being watched with keen interest, not to say anxiety, for if the undisciplined slaves in that island had broken the white man's power, what might not be in store for American slave owners in somewhat the same situation?

Into the cities of Boston, New York, Philadelphia, Baltimore, Charleston, and New Orleans, refugees from the island came flooding, bringing wild tales of terrorism, burning, killing and looting. Ten thousand fled in a convoy from the fire at Cap Français in June, 1792. The following year, five thousand came to New York, not to mention those who found asylum in other cities of the United States.

This rush of suddenly impoverished newcomers placed a great burden on the States. Special sums were voted by the legislatures for their aid—a practical expression of gratitude to a people that only a few years before had given great help to the American cause. By the end of 1794, over three thousand refugees from Saint-Domingue had been the recipients of Federal assistance. Individual cities also helped, and a house of hospitality was set up on Vesey Street in New York to shelter refugees. Over a hundred were living in this place in 1794.

The members of the Bérard household now found themselves surrounded by a whole colony of persons they had known on the island. At the same time there was coming into this country a growing stream of refugees from the French Revolution on the Continent.

Pierre's hairdressing work was soon to associate him, either directly or indirectly, with many famous exiles. One of his patrons, Angelica Schuyler Church, wife of John Barker Church, a wealthy Englishman living in New York, helped many noted personages to reach America. She was the daughter of General Philip Schuyler of Saratoga fame and the sister-in-law of Alexander Hamilton. Her daughter Catherine, later Mrs. Peter Cruger, was to become one of

Pierre's closest friends.

Among those indebted to the beautiful and petulant Angelica Church for their freedom were such refugees from France as Talleyrand and Beaumetz, but it was unlikely that she enjoyed any warm expressions of gratitude from them. Charles Maurice de Talleyrand-Périgord was seldom known to smile or to speak pleasantly to anyone. Passionless, sarcastic, stony-faced, this unfrocked bishop with the club foot was later to wield tremendous power as Napoleon's minister of foreign affairs, and Victor Hugo was to write of him that "during thirty years from the interior of his palace, from the interior of his thoughts, he had almost controlled Europe."

Beaumetz had been a deputy in the French National Assembly. And there was Saint Mémin, famous for his collection of American engravings; the author Volney; Colombe, one-time aide-de-camp to Lafayette. Now they all sought the safety of American soil.

Lafayette himself, at the height of the Terror, was a prisoner in Austria. Madame Lafayette, fearful for the life of their son, begged President Washington to receive him in the United States. George Washington Lafayette came and stayed as a guest of the Alexander Hamiltons for some time.

And in the backwoods of Pennsylvania a huge log cabin was built, three stories high, of ten-inch logs hewed and dragged by rough workers probably unaware of their role in a side show of history. For the cabin was intended as a haven for the queen of France, Marie Antoinette, should she have the chance to exchange the luxuries of a besieged palace for the free air of a rude wilderness shelter.

In Philadelphia, a royalist refugee, Monsieur Gatereau, started to publish a newspaper for the new arrivals. The

Courrier de la France et des Colonies lasted less than a year, due to financial difficulties. From October 15, 1795, to March 1, 1796, it was printed on the press of Moreau de Saint Méry. Its continued absorption with French parliamentary debates reflected the interests of its readers who looked hopefully to Paris for redress of their woes. It was a futile hope, for in France the Terror was growing hourly. Soon it would devour even its instigators—Robespierre, Danton, and others. The guillotine was scarcely ever still.

In the evenings a group of the more intellectual refugees would gather around the stove in the little store of Moreau de Saint Méry, companions in exile, talking of past glories and present disappointments over their bottles of good old Madeira. Saint Méry was a natural pivot for their restless mental energies. A relentless observer and perennial diarist, his history of Saint-Domingue still provides our most detailed picture of the colony, and in his volume *Voyage aux Etats-Unis de l'Amérique, 1793-1798,* we find the most candid and complete account of all he saw and thought during his days in New York, Philadelphia, and other American cities.

Born in Martinique, Moreau de Saint Méry had been educated in France and had practiced law at Cap Français in Saint-Domingue. Back in Paris, during the Revolution, he had been made president of the Paris electors and after the fall of the Bastille, had virtually governed Paris for a short time. His fall came when he incurred the wrath of Robespierre, and he made a most dramatic escape, arriving just ahead of his pursuers on the boat at Le Havre, while his loyal friends carried his half-finished dinner aboard after him.

Through the eyes of Moreau, we know what Pierre saw— the scenes of New York streets, the life of its residents—as he went about the city, calling at the homes of his customers or shopping for his mistress. He heard the people of New York, by and large so favorable to the French revolutionary cause, give expressions to their sentiments by singing the *Çaira* and the *Marseillaise* in their own Independence Day parades. But not all were on the side of the Revolution. There were some, among the parishioners of St. Peter's for example, who had recognized the need for reforms in France but could not countenance the excesses of the Revolution.

This church, to which the Bérards and their slaves belonged, was the only Catholic parish in the city at the time. It had been built in 1785 by a group of twenty- three Catholics under the leadership of Hector Saint Jean de Crevecoeur, the French consul in New York and the author of that immensely popular book on life in the New World being read by all enlightened Europeans, *Letters from an American Farmer.*

A young slave, an ordinary hairdresser, would not have been expected to play a role in the momentous happenings of those days. Yet many of them took place at close range, and Pierre's keen eyes took in many curious, thought-provoking impressions. He would always remember the day in 1790 that De Crevecoeur's daughter America was married to Louis Guillaume Otto, Count of Mosloy, when, at St. Peter's, among other notables, Thomas Jefferson was a witness of the ceremony. The young bridegroom Otto was the one who, later on, as Napoleon's minister in Vienna, would arrange another historic marriage—that of the Emperor to Marie Louise, Archduchess of Austria.

Chapter 8

News from St. Domingue

IN company with her fellow exiles, Marie Bérard had always looked upon her New York sojourn as a temporary interruption in life's journey, a kind of overnight stop en route home, inconvenient but transient. Like the others, she had not been prepared to settle down and remain in the United States indefinitely. And with them she snatched at bits of news and rumor that came to the city via the shipping vessels, wringing from them the last drops of hope and consolation.

In Saint-Domingue Toussaint L'Ouverture had, by 1794, managed to bring about a kind of order, albeit a despotic one. He forced the slaves back to the plantations, but now the owners were compelled to share their profits with the slaves. France accepted his control of the island for some time; there was no alternative. Some of the former landowners now began to return to try to claim their property, and in some cases they were successful for a time in doing so, for L'Ouverture's idealism was tempered by a very practical desire to maintain the economy of his country and he realized the plantations must be kept up. Few indeed of his followers were prepared to take over such a task.

Marie Bérard's sisters, Marie Anne Dessource and Adeline Bossard, were among those who decided to return, and Marie Bouquement, their faithful nurse, went back with them. For Pierre's mistress, the parting was painful, but again all believed it would be but for a short time.

Only disappointment awaited the travelers. They had not realized from a distance how disfigured was the face of their beautiful country from its battle wounds. Everywhere the tragic dramas of war's aftermath were being played, with broken families, motherless children, childless mothers. Everyone was uprooted, unsettled. Letters written with the fading ink of fading hopes lay unanswered, and the names of many loved ones were called over and over, but in vain.

For some reason the Bérard and Bossard estates were not restored to their owners, and Marie Anne and Adeline never even saw their plantation home after their return to the island.

The three sisters agreed to draw up the papers giving Marie Bouquement her legal freedom. The document, dated January 20, 1796, states she was liberated "in recompense for the attachment she has shown us, since the troubles that have afflicted Saint-Domingue, and (we) release her from all service due us."

That was a mere formality, for actually Marie Bouquement's attentions were needed now more than ever before. Marie Anne and Adeline, their health impaired by New York's more rigorous climate, and their spirits crushed by the fruitless homecoming so long anticipated as an event of unparalleled joy, became desperately ill. Marie

Bouquement remained with them, doing all she could to relieve their sufferings, but they did not live long. Soon the sad news had to be sent to Marie Bérard back in New York. It was the second time death had come to her in a letter from Saint-Domingue. She felt her desolation was complete.

She wrote sorrowfully to beseech her nurse, Marie Bouquement, to return to her. It is a pathetic letter, like that of a child to a mother who has abandoned it.

> *How, my dear Marie, is this the way you keep your promise? You told me you would write to me as soon as you reached the Cape. Everyone has written but I find no little note from you. Have you forgotten me, my dear Mémin? This thought makes me sad. I was sorry to part with you, but I would not tell you all I felt lest you should have changed your mind and passed the cold winter here. So now you are at the Cape.*

> *I hear you reached there after a voyage of thirty days. Were you ill, my dear Mémin? How are you now? I am impatient to hear from you. Tell me news of your children.*

> *If it had not been for the last intelligence, we should by this time have been at the Cape; as soon as the French troops arrive, we shall return.*

(Always there were rumors from France that a military expedition would eventually set out to wrest control of the island from Toussaint l'Ouverture.)

> *If you are not well off, come back to me and we will all go to St. Domingue together. You know that you are a second mother to me. I shall never forget all you have done for my poor sisters, and if efforts could have saved*

*anyone, I should, now have them all. . . But God has so
ordered it, and His will be done! Ah, dear Mémin, your
religion will support you under all your sufferings —
never abandon it!*

*Adieu, write me soon, or I shall think you do not love
me any longer. I am always as you used to call me,*

your Bonté

Mémin—Bonté—such pet names were common among
the slaves and their owners. In this letter, so full of tenderness
for her nurse, Marie Bérard revealed her suffering at the loss
of her sisters.

Marie Bouquement, stranded at Cap Français, and unable,
because of the country's internal disorder, to go inland even
to visit Saint Marc, was torn between two decisions. She
knew she was needed by her former mistress in New York,
yet she still had hope of finding her daughter, Adèle, missing
since the uprising. She decided to stay on a little longer before
giving up the search. But several years passed and Adele
could not be found. It is probable she was not even alive at
that time.

But some of the slaves in Saint-Domingue remained on
the old plantations, under owners approved by the governor-
general. Zénobie, Pierre's grandmother, was one of these.
She was still at L'Artibonite, but evidently her circumstances
were none too happy, for her occasional letters to Pierre had
a doleful ring.

She was still, however, the family letter writer, and her
awkwardly scrawled notes, filled with repetitious phrases of
effusive affection, were Pierre's only source of information
about his relatives in the islands. Her grammar was

convulsive, her spelling abominable and her script all but illegible. When it came to news her style was cryptic, leaving much to Pierre's imagination.

"Your mother had a child. The baby is dead," she wrote once. Or again, "Your father and grandfather are jealous because you didn't send them any gifts." Her own wants were stated quite clearly, "I need a pair of scissors." Pierre responded dutifully to all these requests, and never complained of the sketchy reports addressed by the aged matriarch to "The Citizen Toussaint, residing in New York."

Pierre's work as a hairdresser increased almost daily. His apprenticeship was about to end, for Mr. Merchant conceded that the time had come for another arrangement to be made. One day the master coiffeur called on Madame Bérard and told her he was unable to teach Pierre anything more—her slave knew all his tricks, and more besides. The fifty dollars agreed upon by Jean Bérard for the apprenticeship was in fact long overdue. If Madame would kindly pay, then Pierre would be free to start off on his own—an equal, perhaps even a rival, in the trade.

But Madame Bérard was of course unable to pay; she did not have the fifty dollars. However, by this time she was used to making excuses, and she managed to send Mr. Merchant away with some vague promise of an early remittance.

It was like Pierre to know that the hairdresser had come, and why. As Mr. Merchant was leaving, no doubt a little provoked at being put off by the wealthy Madame Bérard, Pierre met him in the hallway, and followed him outside.

"The matter of payment for my apprenticeship—"

"Yes? What about it, Pierre?" He was really a bit annoyed.

"It is my wish to pay the debt myself, if you will accept it in small portions, as I earn it," Pierre suggested.

Mr. Merchant agreed to being paid on the installment plan. He knew he would get his money in good time, for Pierre could be trusted. Besides, Mr. Merchant knew Pierre now had plenty of customers—more, perhaps, than would be good for Mr. Merchant's own trade.

This was well, for now Pierre was the sole support of the Bérard home. A slave in name only, he remained always in the background, the unobtrusive sustainer, both spiritually and materially. He disciplined himself firmly in the matter of spending money, buying for himself only the basic necessities and turning over nearly the whole of his income to Madame Bérard. Even the share of his earnings he was entitled to keep he contributed toward the expenses of the household. He insisted on one rule he had early made for himself "and I have never departed from it through life— that of not incurring a debt, and scrupulously paying on the spot for everything I purchased."

This discipline would always remain with him. In his papers there is evidence of sound order and efficiency in money matters. He filed away his receipts, notes from friends repaying money he had lent them, records of financial transactions, however trivial, and carefully kept them among his voluminous correspondence.

Each day would begin for Pierre with six o'clock Mass at St. Peter's Church. Then he would go to buy the groceries and other supplies for the day. Perhaps to the Fly Market, down on the East Side near Wall and Water streets, where were sold the fresh fruit and vegetables that had been brought over before daylight by boat from Brooklyn farms. Or he might go to the Catherine Market, famed for its fish, which some people claimed was the best in the world. The nearest marketplace for Pierre was the Oswego, at The Broadway near Maiden Lane. Often he had to make the rounds of several of these markets to complete his purchases. After this he would go home again with the supplies, not forgetting a special treat for his mistress—some reminder of her tropical homeland, perhaps oranges or bananas, pearls of great price in the new metropolis although commonplace back home in Saint Marc.

Only after Mass and shopping would he stop for breakfast, a hurried one certainly, for it would soon be time for his hairdressing appointments to begin. Although New York was so much smaller in area in those days, he had still to do all his traveling on foot, and it took time to cover the distance to the homes where his customers awaited his attention before officially beginning their day.

Pierre had first become a hairdresser in the age of powder and pomatum, when hair arrangements were immense, disproportionate structures, piled high on feminine heads. Even when powder was relinquished, hair styles had remained architectural. With the French Revolution had come wigs or perukes, adopted quickly by American ladies of fashion. Now heads were completely shaved and blondes and brunettes became interchangeable by virtue of the wig.

During Pierre's long career many styles succeeded one another in rapid succession, but he proved equal to all of fashion's vagaries. His knowledge of the current styles won him wide acclaim in the circle of society. Soon he had all the trade of the French ladies of New York as well as of many English-speaking customers who grew to admire his skill.

When the day of wigs had passed, the hair styles became more natural. For a time the hair was worn cropped, drawn up over the head, the short strands curled over the top.

Then came the Grecian style. Pierre arranged them all with humorous acceptance, laughing at fashion's whims at the same time that he catered to them.

In a book of reminiscences, *Echoes of a Belle,* written many years later under the implausible pseudonym of Ben Shadow, a lady who knew Pierre gave a quaint picture of him at work:

> *Alice [the author] was seated before her glass, a fashion-able hairdresser had been sent for; and the illustrious Toussaint, with his good tempered face, small earrings, and white teeth, entered the room, his tall figure arrayed in a spotless apron.*
>
> *The curling tongs were heated, and there was a perfume of scorched paper as Toussaint commenced operations. Oh, those cruel scissors, they had no mercy upon the beautiful hair. What an execution! Alice shrank from the sight of her tortured head which, in a hundred "papillotes" seemed to stand upon end in every direction; whilst Luna held the brushes and heated the tongs, in silent amazement at this curious phenomenon; but to Mrs. Vere [Alice's mother], Toussaint's sable face was a most refreshing sight.*
>
> *The elaborate "coiffure" was completed, and Toussaint enchanted with his "chef d'oeuvre a la Valière." Alice thought herself a rival to Miss Tilton; she did not question the style; it was the fashion, and that was enough.*

Pierre's was a long day, sometimes sixteen hours, all of it spent standing—either walking from house to house or behind the chair of a customer. When he did come home, it was not to rest. He always knew he would find Madame

Bérard sitting sadly in her shadowed room, perhaps even forgetting to light the lamps, unless Rosalie had done it for her. He would tell her stories of the day's happenings to amuse and cheer her. Then she would smile a little and be pleased as a child over some small surprise he had brought, some little iced cakes from the confectionery, or a bit of that recent and exotic French import—ice cream.

As time passed, Marie Bérard's melancholy had deepened, and Pierre saw the dangers of her state of mind. He realized she must live not only on his money, but, more important, on his sturdy faith.

"I knew her," he said later, "full of life and gaiety, richly dressed and entering into amusements with animation.

"Now the scene was so changed, and it was so sad to me. Sometimes when an invitation came, I would succeed in persuading her to accept it and I would come in the evening to dress her hair. Then I contrived a little surprise for her. When I had finished I would present her the glass and say:

" 'Madame, how do you like it?'

"Oh, how pleased she was! I had placed in her hair some beautiful flower—perhaps a japonica, perhaps a rose, remarkable for its rare species, which I had purchased at a greenhouse and concealed until the time had arrived."

Sometimes Pierre would bring her pen and paper and urge her to write out invitations to a few close friends. When they were ready he would go and deliver them at their various homes. When the evening of the party came, Pierre would be there, gay and resplendent in his red jacket, serving the guests with his usual good humor. No one guessed that it was the slave, not the hostess, who had provided the refreshments.

Little things—a special flower, a small gathering of friends. Yet he understood what these can mean in a life threatened with complete despondency. He knew his mistress' exquisite tastes and he could appreciate her dismay at the loss of all those luxuries which from childhood she had grown to expect.

In 1801 the day finally came when the vast French fleet sailed toward Saint-Domingue, the tricolor flying proudly. General Leclerc, husband of Napoleon's sister Josephine, was in command. Now, it was thought, the rebels of Saint Domingue, especially their leader L'Ouverture, would be forced to submit once and for all.

But the native leaders were ready when the ships neared their coast. Toussaint, Dessalines, and Henri Christophe, with all their forces, met the French attack with a fierce and potent defense. Leclerc was taken by surprise. He had expected no difficulty in routing a ragged and undisciplined mob of former slaves. Staggered by their well-organized repulse, Leclerc hesitated, and in that moment a second enemy attacked: yellow fever began rapidly to decimate his ranks. His proud force was wiped out almost overnight. It was the first of three great defeats history had in store for Napoleon. Years later would come the retreat from Russia and the Battle of Waterloo.

But Leclerc's mission was not an utter failure. He had managed by stratagem to carry out one of Napoleon's dearest schemes—the capture of Toussaint L'Ouverture. He was put on board a French ship and carried away to France, to a dungeon in the Jura Mountains. There he was to die, in 1803, in a land of snow and ice, in a frozen silence that all but obscured memories of the tropic sun.

Meanwhile, on the island, Dessalines, Christophe, and Pétion carried on as well as they could, but without the sure judgments of their true leader.

In the last hours of battle, Leclerc, seeing no hope of rallying his men, pleaded with Napoleon to send reinforcements if they were to hold the island. But none came, and at last Leclerc himself succumbed to the fever and all was lost for France.

It was then that the exultant people of Saint-Domingue declared their country a republic, abandoned the hated French name and called it instead by its ancient title "Haiti" —mountainous land. The second republic of the Western Hemisphere was established.

CHAPTER 9

A NEW MARRIAGE

ONE EVENING in early 1802, Madame Bérard sat gazing at her reflection in her dessing-table mirror. Just behind her chair, Pierre was putting the finishing touches to her dark hair. Her face, usually so pale, glowed with a faint pink tonight, almost a look of health, which had not been hers for many years. And her eyes, usually so dull, had a little of their old sparkle.

"Aren't you through yet, Pierre?" she asked. Her slightly querulous tone belied the smile on her thin face. "The curtain will be going up before I am even ready to leave for the theater."

Pierre smiled patiently. He knew her foibles so well. "Never fear, Madame. The performance never starts on time, you know. You will be early enough." His quick fingers sought to secure the stem of a perfect pink rose atop Madame Bérard's curls. It was one of the first of the season, not quite full-blown, and he had bought it from the florist on his way home that afternoon.

Tonight was one of his mistress's rare evenings away from home. She had accepted an invitation to attend a play—something she seldom could bring herself to do these days.

Pierre's sister Rosalie entered the room just as he had finished his work. He was holding up the mirror for Madame Bérard to admire her new coiffure.

"Monsieur Nicolas is here, Madame," Rosalie announced. "He says not to hurry; there is plenty of time."

Madame Bérard took a last look in the mirror, caught up her little beaded purse and went toward the door. Her dress, of palest pink satin, gave an illusion of youth to her somewhat wasted figure and set off her strikingly white skin. If only her cheeks were not so thin, thought Pierre, as he watched her leave. But at least it would do her good to go out tonight. Monsieur Nicolas was always kind and gentle toward her. He too was a refugee from the island and knew well what it was to lose fortune and friends at one swift blow. Among the little group of refugees who met sometimes at the Bérard home to exchange a small comfort in the news brought by ship from Saint-Domingue, Gabriel Nicolas was certainly the most sympathetic.

That he was almost penniless meant very little in their circle now, for nearly all the French refugees were in the same situation. Only a few had escaped with enough money to buy a modest home, a small business or farm. Most of them were really destitute.

Gabriel, however, was better off than some, for he was an accomplished musician. He could play the violin and piano well enough to earn from time to time a little money in the orchestra pit of the theater. When he worked, he made enough to pay for his meager lodging, and by dining fairly often at the Bérard table he managed to survive.

He had even arranged to hire a carriage for tonight's trip across the town to the theater on John Street. He could not afford it, of course, but he did it because he hoped this would be a very special evening. He had grown very fond of the lonely Marie Bérard—they had so much in common—and he intended to ask her, on the way home, to marry him.

Father Matthew O'Brien performed the wedding ceremony at St. Peter's Church on the 11th day of August, 1802. Evidently he was much impressed by the couple's background, for the record in the parish register is one of the longest entries over a period of twenty years.

> ... I, the undersigned have joined in marriage according to the rites of the Catholic Church, Gabriel Jean Baptiste Désiré Nicolas, citizen of the Isle of Saint-Domingue from the Aquin quarter, and now a resident of New York, a major in age and the legitimate son of Gabriel Jean Désiré Nicolas, former advisor to the Superior Council of Port-au- Prince and Demoiselle Adelaide Sophie de Lenois, citizens of the same quarter, and Demoiselle Adelaide Marie Elisabeth Bossard, resident of the aforesaid Isle of Saint Domingue and the quarter of Marmalade and a native of the parish of Dondon, widow by her first marriage without children to Philippe Pierre Roudanès and in the second marriage, also without children, to Jean Jacques Bérard, citizen of the quarter of Artibonite. The said Demoiselle Marie Elisabeth Bossard, a major in age, being the legitimate daughter of the late Louis Bossard and the late Lady Marie Anne Fleury, citizens of the Isle of Saint-Domingue of the quarter of Marmalade.

The priest must have then paused for a long breath before he signed his name— "M. O'Brien, *unus ex pastoribus Sancti Petri ecclesiae*" —one of the pastors of St. Peter's Church.

So Marie Bérard became Marie Nicolas, and while it was too much for either of them to hope for exuberant happiness after so much adversity, still the companionship removed that worst curse of the exile—loneliness. Gabriel was faithful, conscientious, thoughtful. But he could not earn enough to support the household and so in money matters things went on very much as they had before, with Pierre quietly footing the bills from his now sizable income as a hairdresser.

The Reade Street "family" now included Madame and Monsieur Nicolas; Pierre's sister Rosalie, who attended to the domestic affairs; and, of course, Pierre. Still absent was Marie Bouquement, who had remained at Cap Français in an unsuccessful attempt to find her missing daughter. Marie Nicolas kept pleading for her nurse to return to her, and, in the summer of 1803, Pierre added his persuasions to those of his mistress. He wrote his aunt anxiously:

> Had you written through Monsieur Laferrière, you would have given me great pleasure as well as to Madame. She knows that you are very worried and that you cry each day. She urges you to come here and I do the same. Oh, how happy I would be to see and to embrace you. . . .

And thinking of those of his own family still surviving on the island, he added:

I want you to believe that I love you very much as well
as my sister; give many messages to our whole family.
Tell me how the whole family is. Madame Nicolas' eye is
still sore. All the servants in the house send their greet-
ings . . . Mr. Aubrun Curé (Father O'Brien, pastor of
Saint Peter's Church) often asks me of you.. . .

At last Marie Bouquement gave up her search. She was
bound by ties of love and loyalty to Marie Nicolas, ties no
legal document could ever dissolve. She came back and again
took up her attendance on her former mistress.

We can quickly turn the faded pages of Old St. Peter's
marriage records and see the weddings Gabriel Nicolas
attended as a witness and where he no doubt furnished the
music. His name appears often, and several times that of Jean
Sorbieu, another friend of Pierre's, is there also.

Gabriel's musical talents would have been welcome assets
to any festive occasion. After the religious service was over,
and the wedding guests had enjoyed the customary breakfast,
the dancing would begin to Gabriel's accompaniment on the
violin or the piano.

Those Saint-Domingue weddings must have been joyous
events. Everyone who attended, it seemed, wanted to have his
name on the register, and when a certain number had signed,
it was no doubt up to the officiating priest tactfully to call a
halt to the list of witnesses.

On ordinary evenings, the Reade Street house resounded
often to gay music, just as in the old days. Gabriel and
Pierre would combine their skill to drive Madame Nicolas'
melancholy away. Gabriel always had many stories to tell of
the day's doings at the theater or other places—that is, on the
days when there was work.

What his activities lacked in financial return was made up in excitement, for especially in the theater did he find one of New York's most lively sources of interest. The city's first theater on John Street was where George Washington had so enjoyed the plays, and, what was extremely rare for him, had actually laughed. Now this theater had been augmented by a second, The Park, on Chatham Street, facing what is now City Hall Square.

New York drama had come far since the day in 1787 when Royall Tyler, the first successful American playwright, had presented his comedy, *The Contrast,* in five acts at the John Street Theater. Now, in the early years of the nineteenth century, William Dunlap, local impresario, was ambitiously translating plays from German and French, and bringing a cosmopolitan note to the New York stage. Unlike Tyler, Dunlap had sedulously studied the theater abroad and was trying to capture some of its magic for theater-conscious New Yorkers. Brilliant actors like Junius Booth and John Howard Payne, author of *Home, Sweet Home,* were joining their talents to the dramatic efforts of Fitz-Greene Halleck and others.

Gabriel Nicolas, of course, watched the performances from his chair in the orchestra pit, where he was one of the performers of the *entr'acte* music, mostly the work of French refugees who had mastered their art well. He would bring home tales of the escapades of his fellow-musician, Brillat-Savarin, whose musical talent was combined with an enormous gusto for food.

In Saint-Domingue, the theater had been an integral part of the life of the planters, so Gabriel Nicolas in New York was merely carrying over as participant an enthusiasm he had many times experienced as a spectator in the island colony.

Down there a play might be interrupted by a hurricane or an earthquake. In New York the only unpleasant rumblings were the dark forebodings of puritan minds who thundered against the moral hazards of the stage.

Through his hairdressing work, Pierre was coming into touch with more and more citizens of New York who played a part in both national and international affairs. His customer and friend Catherine Church introduced him to many of those who were interesting themselves in land pioneering in western New York State, Pennsylvania, and even as far west as Ohio.

Bancel de Confoulens had assisted in starting the Scioto colony beside the Ohio River; his son Victor Bancel had become a staunch friend of Pierre's. The Scioto experiment failed, but other similar communities succeeded, at least for a time. One of these was Angelica, founded by Philip Church, Catherine Church's brother, and named in honor of their mother Angelica Schuyler Church. Among those who became interested in the Angelica settlement was the Baron Hyde de Neuville, who had fled to America with his wife to escape Napoleon's displeasure. She was a noted painter of the American scene and among her famous sketches are some showing pioneer life at Angelica. The De Neuvilles for a time conducted a school in New York but later turned it over to Victor Bancel.

The Bancels had been members of the royal guard of Louis XVI of France, and their New York home, first on Harrison Street and later on Anthony Street, was a popular gathering place for the French colony. Pierre went regularly to the Bancel school to cut the children's hair and to help them dress for parties and entertainments, thus further cementing his close ties with the family.

One summer morning in 1804, when Pierre was thirty-eight years old, he was halted en route to one of his appointments by a strange scene on the tree-shaded Broadway. He at once became aware of something tragic when he came upon the crowds pressed along the street, many weeping openly, others struck silent by the sudden and violent death of a public idol. Pierre stood, with the rest of New York's population, to see Alexander Hamilton's funeral cortege pass from the home of John Barker Church in Robinson Street, through Beekman, Pearl, and The Broadway to Trinity Church. The hat and sword of the young statesman rested on his coffin, and just behind it, two white-clad black men led Hamilton's gray horse, a figure of forlorn dignity. Pierre waited until the next carriage had passed, bearing the dead man's family.

As Elizabeth Schuyler Hamilton, erect in her widow's black, rode behind her husband's body, her numbed mind tried to piece together two parts of a picture which did not fit into each other at all. This scene, dreamlike, unreal! And the other one as her husband had stepped out of their home at the Grange but a few days ago. Handsomely dressed, immaculately groomed as usual, he had begun that walk leading him down the steep hill to the broad Hudson and to the boat that idled there, waiting to take him to the heights of Weehawken, to the deadly aim of Aaron Burr, to this. . .

It was a day of calamity, not only for Elizabeth Hamilton, but for the whole nation.

"The death of Hamilton," wrote Henry Adams afterward, "and the Vice-President's flight, with the accessories of a Summer morning, sunlight on rocks and wooden heights, tranquil river and distant city, and behind all, the dark background of moral gloom, double treason and political despair still stand as the most dramatic moment in the early politics of the union."

Pierre, as he witnessed this somber moment, murmured a prayer for the soul of his fellow-islander. Hamilton's quixotic star had first risen, like Pierre's, in the West Indies. Although Pierre may have known this, he could not have foreseen that the Schuyler and Hamilton families, both so famous in American history, would be linked again by marriage, and through them the name of an obscure slave, Pierre Toussaint, would be woven into the fabric of several noted lives.

CHAPTER 10

CONSOLER OF THE AFFLICTED

Pierre's position in the Nicolas home required of him unbelievable discretion and tact. To shield his sensitive and gentle mistress from further pain and humiliation— that was his life. To the world outside he was still a slave, yet he had taken on a far more responsible role than his legal status required. What was even stranger in those days, he had established himself in an independent business and was regularly employed in many households, while still remaining the property of one.

He could not fail to attract notice in the small community that was then New York. People suspected or tacitly accepted the fact that he was really the support of his mistress' household. But to advert to this in his presence would have been unthinkable. Pierre's dignity, completely independent of his social status, imposed reserve even where it did not ordinarily exist. If Marie Nicolas needed a wall against an unkind world, he was that wall. Not a word of her distress would ever pass his lips during her lifetime. And those who might have been tempted to make conversational capital of her predicament held their tongues because of something Pierre Toussaint did, or was.

But charity like this could not be contained under one roof. He had always possessed a keen perception of others' needs and the ability to do something about them. Even from the few dollars he kept to buy his supplies and working uniforms he had managed to contribute to relieving the distress of a great number of persons.

And this could not be kept secret. More and more they began to think of Pierre when troubles came. Somehow it seemed natural to come to him for help.

In Pierre's correspondence, there were many begging letters from persons in all stations of life—from some who were slaves like himself, from hard-hit aristocrats, from priests and missionaries. And from those unknown and insignificant little persons whom history is always maiming accidentally as it brushes by.

Let us take Madame le Due. There are hundreds of Madame le Dues scattered throughout the world. We never notice them. We would not have noticed her either, had she not chosen to appeal to Pierre in her troubles.

She wrote in the third person, making the tragedy sound quite matter of fact and free of tears.

Persuaded that the misfortunes which afflict Madame Le Due, formerly a resident of Port-au-Prince, cannot be a matter of indifference to feeling hearts who learn that this unfortunate mother has the care of three young children, that she now lives in this city bereft of means to

give them the necessities of life, whose father was mas-
sacred by the Negroes, she thinks that even though she
keeps hidden the terrible details of her tragedy, you will
be moved to help her according to your means.

It is dated June 3, 1804. At the bottom of the page, some names of those who responded, among them: "Toussaint— $2.00." An insignificant sum, hardly worth noting.

Yet the widow Le Due was white, and Pierre was black —as black as the man who had murdered her husband in the Saint-Domingue fighting. She had been born free, only to become a prisoner of inexorable circumstance. Pierre had been born in bondage, at liberty only in spiritual realms. So she becomes a symbol to those who came to know Pierre and his charity that transcended race, politics, religion—every barrier known to divide man from man.

It was his peculiar gift and people were not long in discovering it. Few days went by without someone handing in a little note for him at the door of the Nicolas house, calling to his attention some charitable cause.

Some came from his fellow-parishioners at St. Peter's:

Do me the service, my dear Toussaint, of recommending
to St. Peter's Benevolent Society, Madame Hayes who lives
at No. 82 Wooster Street, in the court-yard. What is most
necessary to her is some firewood. This poor woman is
suffering greatly from consumption. If you wish to stop at
my house, I shall remit to you my subscription.

M. DuBerceau

Sometimes the projects he undertook for others required continued time and effort.

> *Mr. Tousan: You mentioned to me this morning that*
> *you would get me some scholars. I hope you will not*
> *forget me as I am very needy.*
>   *From Miss Gillingham, and please to accept of her*
> *thanks.*

Tutoring was a popular way for genteel ladies to tide themselves over an embarrassing financial crisis, and in his daily work, Pierre was now in a most favorable position to seek help for those in need. He was going into the homes of some of New York's wealthiest citizens. More and more he was being received as a trusted friend and adviser as well as master of the comb and curling iron. He had a custom of soliciting a few dollars here and there from his customers and turning them over to various welfare funds. Each sum was carefully noted down, with the donor's name. Receipts were given and records kept of these individual fund-raising campaigns.

It was not always money that he gave. There were other gifts—consoling the afflicted, admonishing the sinner. A man might be poor in diverse ways. There were those *"in prison, and you visited me— "* as we gather from a tiny scrap of paper, a very moving plea.

> *My dear Toussaint:*
>   *It is to you, consoler of the unfortunate, that I appeal,*
> *to beg you, to plead with you to come to see me in this*
> *sad place. I have written to many persons, but in vain!*
> *I beg you to come and see me. Take a carriage. I will*
> *pay the fare. God will repay you for this kindness which*
> *I ask of you. I have many things to tell you. I beg you,*
> *do not fail me. I await you today or tomorrow, or even*
> *later.*
>
>   *Your unhappy friend,*
>   *L. Emmerling Bellevue Prison.*

His remarkable sympathy led him often to the side of the bereaved. One day he went to call on a lady to whom death had just dealt a heavy blow.

Someone asked him afterward, "What did you say to the poor woman?"

"Nothing," Toussaint answered simply. "I could only take her hand and weep with her, and then I went away. There was nothing to be said." Only God, he knew, could speak at such a time. But his compassionate manner, the faith and love so evident in his few words somehow managed to convey comfort to others.

He was also able at times to ransom the captive—captives, that is, of a system that bought and sold men as other material commodities. His records show that he put up money for some of his slave friends to buy their freedom.

But he never made any move to secure his own. He must have believed intensely in personal liberty, for he often lent money to other slaves for this purpose. When he first began to earn money as a hairdresser, he had begun to set aside a small amount regularly to buy the freedom of his sister Rosalie.

Many of the impoverished French families were glad now to sell their slaves, for they needed the money. Daily papers carried frequent notices of slave sales. Occasionally a slave would be given his freedom as a reward for unusually loyal service, or because the master simply could no longer support him. But many others bought their freedom on the installment plan. Sometimes the payments ran on for many years.

Around the turn of the century a law had been passed declaring the children of slaves freedmen after they reached a certain age. The slaves in New York, jubilant over this move toward emancipation, planned a huge celebration on July 5, 1800. They came to ask if Pierre would lead the triumphal parade. He declined politely, wishing them every success, but adding: "I owe my freedom to my mistress, not to the state." But apparently Marie Nicolas never thought of giving him legally what he possessed actually: the status of a free man.

Pierre never participated in political demonstrations. Much later on, someone would ask him if he were an abolitionist. And he would shake his head sadly.

"They don't know what I have seen," he said. "They have not seen blood flow as I have."

It was his only known reference to the Saint-Domingue uprising, and one of the few statements he was ever known to have made on the subject of slavery.

One of Pierre's friends, Jean Nelson, was evidently among those whose freedom was financed by Pierre. Nelson received his papers on May 3, 1805, probably with a down payment of Pierre's money, and he was still paying at the end of almost eleven years:

> *September 4, 1816: I, the undersigned, acknowledge having received from Mr. Nelson, the sum of sixty-three piastres on account of one hundred and fifty. Mr. Nelson has promised to give me this capital in conformity with our arrangements made before witnesses in this city of New York on Sept. 18, 1804.*
>
> *L. Frenois*

Faith and fortitude, money, firewood, freedom—so many waited nowadays to take the gifts Pierre brought them. They gave little in return. Sometimes a thank you, sometimes not.

There were two young men, members of a French family, who remind us of the ten lepers of the Gospel. After much difficulty and hard work, Pierre finally succeeded in finding for them work that they needed very badly. Afterward, unwilling to be reminded of their former straits, they pointedly avoided him.

"I'm glad they are so well off," he commented without rancor. "They do not need me any more."

That was the way of things. Pierre understood human nature. He looked for no rewards. It was his object to forget immediately any injuries he suffered. If he were ever lonely, shaken or uncertain, there was only one who knew it: Juliette Noel. She too had come from Haiti. Her mother, Claudine Gaston, was a nurse with a French family.

Pierre had bought Juliette's freedom when they first met, when she was only fifteen and he was thirty-five. Although she was so much younger, her understanding of Pierre had grown deeper over the years. With others he kept his counsel; with her he could always speak his heart. They both knew now that they loved one another. Someday—but they must be patient.

Pierre was not yet free to marry. He was still the slave of the helpless Marie Nicolas, as well as her main support. But this would not go on much longer. The last light of hope had left his mistress's eyes. By early 1807 she had grown too tired of disappointments. The faint belief that the French government might indemnify her for her lost estates she knew now as but a passing mirage. She knew that she was indeed poor, had been, and would be poor. And what was more painful, she could never repay one penny to the slave who had cared for her with such devotion these twenty years.

Coming in each evening, Pierre found it hard to smile and be gay when he saw his mistress. How she had aged! Not only from sorrow, but from sickness as well. He forced himself to sound cheerful.

"Does Madame wish anything just now?"

She sat, propped up with pillows, in her chair near the fire, her silver pencil resting on a small pad in her lap. She was never without her pencil in these days, for a throat ailment prevented her from speaking. Her fingers moved over the little sheet of paper. She wrote many of these notes every day. It was her only way of making her thoughts known.

"Dites-moi les nouvelles, Pierre."

Always the same request, night after night. It meant nothing really. Marie Nicolas was not truly interested any more in what happened in the world outside her room. It was only when Pierre was there talking of his day, what he had done, whom he had seen, of one thing and another of no great import, that she felt stronger. He bolstered her weakened spirits as no one else could.

Rosalie and Marie Bouquement waited on the sick woman with loving care. Gabriel Nicolas, deeply devoted, stayed by her side. Still it was Pierre on whom she leaned the most.

One evening she seemed to have something special on her mind. As Pierre talked to her, she was toying with her pencil, deep lines of worry on her fragile face. At last she handed him the little scrap on which she had written.

"Mémin — you'll always watch over her, won't you?"

She must know then, Pierre thought, that she would not live much longer. He began to pray for faith, not only for himself but for her.

"Do not worry, Madame," he replied calmly. "My aunt is very dear to me . . ."

Madame Nicolas tried to write again.

"Call her . . . please . . . to help me . . . to bed."

The handwriting trailed off. She was really too weak to finish.

Pierre closed the door softly.

Chapter 11

The Gift of Freedom

In Saint Domingue—now Haiti —Dessalines ruled, but no longer simply as Dessalines. He had had himself crowned Jean Jacques the First, following a custom set by another self-styled emperor, Napoleon.

In the new empire, blacks and mulattoes were soon divided—the blacks in the north, under Dessalines and the mulattoes in the south, under his rival, Pétion. But the true enemy was the white man.

Dessalines, "the Tiger," stalked his prey with savage fury. From his lair the order went out to every black soldier to hunt the quarry down wherever he lay hiding, in field or home or forest. When the victims had been herded together outside the town of Port-au-Prince, Dessalines rode out to view the slaughter. Casually, he gave the signal, and then he watched them die.

He had sworn to ride in blood the length of that once beautiful country, but he did not live to carry this out. His subjects were sickened by his cruelty and he fell on the road, slain, it is said, by one of his own men.

Henri Christophe then took up the leadership of the blacks. From his incredible fortress La Ferriere, rising like a ship's prow from the craggy heights of an inaccessible mountain on the northern plain, he likewise ruled with an iron hand. King Henry—crowned at his own request.

The few whites who had been able to escape fled to Cuba. Some of the peace-loving blacks and *gens de couleur* also went there, in despair over the violence and terrorism in their land.

Pierre's older sister, Marie-Louise Pacaud, and her husband were among those who reached Cuba. Pierre wrote his sister there on May 28, 1807:

> *Madam:*
>
> *I received the letter you did me the pleasure of writing. It reached me too late to answer as soon as I should have liked. I am very surprised that my brother whom you told me was in Saint Iago isn't with you. I don't know what could have led him there except the evacuation of Port-au-Prince. Do me the kindness of telling me with whom he stays so that I can send him something or have him come here. I am very unhappy that your son is not with you. If I have the good fortune to meet him in this country, I will do anything I can to be of service to him.*
>
> *I send you the three packages of tobacco you asked of me. If you need anything else, you have only to ask. I will send you whatever you need. I wish you perfect health and am yours very sincerely. Give my respects to Mr. Pacaud.*
>
> *Your very humble and obedient servant*
> *Toussaint.*

He must have followed up this letter with another one a few days later, for she writes to him on July 12 of the same year.

I received safely your letter dated June 8, my dear
Toussaint, through Miss Frangoise, as well as the two
packages of tobacco. I thank you. I am going to pass
on your letter to Toussaint [Pierre's brother]. He is 25
leagues from here but I have learned that he is well.
When you wish to write him, always send your letter
through me. I am thankful for the news you send me
of my son, Victor. If you can get his address in Paris,
write to him and reproach him for giving no sign of life.
I have no news from Antonie [her daughter]. We must
hope that one day, I shall have the happiness of seeing
you again. I miss Jeanne and Saint [evidently family pet
names for Rosalie and Marie Bouquement]. I advise all
three of you to go on with your good behavior so that
you will be worthy of Madame's kindness. Mr. Pacaud
greets you. We are very miserable here and live with
great difficulty. I wonder when we shall get out of this
sad position. I wish you good health and am always

Your good sister
Marie-Louise.

P.S. I have no news of Tonette and Gran'mère.

Later, she wrote to Pierre, saying that his brother was in
Cuba near La Trinité. She had received news that Ursule and
Zénobie were in great need. She argued against his going
back to the island. All was confusion there and the greatest
disorder prevailed.

Pierre would go on for years trying to get in touch with
his family at Haiti. His friend Jean-Baptiste Nelson, who had
returned to the island, wrote him saying that another friend
had thought he had seen Ursule in Port-au-Prince. On the
next trip to the town he hoped to check on the story.

Marie Nicolas lay quietly in her bed, her eyes closed. There was no sun in the room but in her mind the sun was shining brighter than in many a year. Its warm light poured like gold over the windowpanes, and she was back in her valley where the cold winds never blew.

She was a child again, on her father's big plantation, a little girl running under the sun-drenched palm trees, among forests of gay tropical blossoms. Playing with her sisters on the broad verandas of their home. Dressing for a ball in a gown of sheerest muslin, like fairy cloth, printed with exquisite rosebuds.

Oh, she would be the prettiest tonight. She would be the most graceful of all the dancers. All the young men would bow before her, murmuring compliments and smiling their flattering smiles. And she held out her hand, answering prettily, with just the proper gravity, for she was only a child-widow at this time, one whom sorrow could touch but lightly. It was life, not death, the music was celebrating. She was searching among the guests for one . . . within the magic circle of the colored lanterns in the garden, flickering now on the dark faces of the players, now on the gay whirling dancers. Her heart was beating furiously . . . Jean, Jean, but where was Jean? Surely he would be here tonight, for he had promised. Yes, there he was, coming now, walking toward her with his sure stride, splendidly handsome in his new Paris clothes.

"I thought you weren't coming, Jean."

"Not coming! But I promised. Of course I've come. I'll always come, Marie."

Yes, of course. How foolish of her to doubt him. Jean would always be there beside her, holding her hand. She opened her eyes very slowly.

"Jean—"

But the face beside her was another's.

"What is it, dear?"

Painfully, she returned to her shade-drawn room. Gabriel, of course. She remembered now. She turned her head, ever so slightly, to see the other chair, the one near the door. Pierre sat quietly, his book opened on his lap. He looked up, sensing that she had wakened and was watching him.

"Shall I read, Madame?"

She nodded wearily. His voice quieted her. She began to drift again. The music was still playing, but far off this time, and something kept interrupting it. Something lay in the bottom of her mind, setting off jangling discords. What was it? Something . . . she wanted to do. With a great effort she opened her eyes again. Pierre paused a moment in his reading. Pierre! Oh, now she knew.

With tremendous will power she roused herself and focused attention on what she had to do. Just one more thing, and then back to L'Artibonite and its carefree joy forever.

She felt her life had been something of a failure, from a human viewpoint. It had been bitter to be forced to go on year after year, always being the taker, when one has been born to be a giver. But she still had one thing to give to the slave who had been so generous, so steadfast.

To Gabriel, sitting patiently by her bedside, she tried to communicate her plan. By sign and painful whisper she managed to convey the idea. He must go for the lawyer, at once, so that Pierre's freedom papers could be drawn up.

Gabriel looked down at her with a gesture of protest. Preparing such a document was a long-drawn-out affair requiring the presence of witnesses. Such an exertion would be too much of a strain on her failing strength.

He placed his hand over hers soothingly.

"Don't worry, dear. We'll take care of that. Whatever you want shall be done."

But she could not leave this for others to do.

"Now—now," she whispered. "Hurry, please."

"Please don't distress yourself," Gabriel insisted. "Whatever you want us to do, you have only to ask—"

But she insisted. Papers were sent for, and lawyer and witnesses. All must be done according to forms laid down by the French government.

It is a pretentious document: *"Extract of the Minutes of the Chancellor of the French Commissariat in New York,"* inscribed with many flourishes, and sealed with the crowned eagle of the French Empire.

> *I, the undersigned, Elisabeth Bossard, wife of Monsieur Gabriel Nicolas, declare, with the consent of Mr. Nicolas, my husband, that my intention is that Pierre Toussaint my slave shall be and live free of all servitude and I consent that he enjoy liberty like any other freed-man, that this present act be given all the public authenticity that it may have. Made at New York, July 2, 1807.*

Then followed the signatures of Marie, Gabriel, and the witnesses. One was Pierre's good friend, Jean Sorbieu, a parishioner of St. Peter's. The other "Fr. Brun" may have been one of St. Peter's priests. The document ends with several formal certifications affixed by the French chancellor, Jean Baptiste Anne Marie Lombart.

When this was done, the sick woman lay back on her pillows, exhausted. She had tried to thank Pierre for all he had done for her, but that was impossible.

"I have only done my duty," he protested.

"You have done much more. You have been everything to me. There is no remuneration on earth for such service."

Instead, she begged Almighty God to reward Pierre, in His own way. She had given Toussaint a little miniature of

herself to keep as a souvenir. At the end, she spoke again of
Marie Bouquement, her beloved nurse.

"As you love my memory, never forsake her. If ever you
should leave the country—let her go with you."

Then she asked to be alone with the priest. Life had been
a singular struggle. Now it was death that came peaceably.

Pierre, through his sorrow, was thankful. After so many
years of trial, she had kept a strong hold on her faith to the
very end. An answer to his prayers.

And she had left him free!

"I asked only to make her comfortable," he said of her,
"and I bless God that she never knew a want."

CHAPTER 12

THE PLAGUE

It was August, a tense, uneasy month in New York.

Each year it was the same, the fearful suspense hanging over the humid streets. Everyone waiting to see if *it* would come again this year. And when it came, which was very often, a whisper that was more like a shudder ran through the city, from the Battery to the Bowery Road, from the busy East River docks to the big wharves of the Hudson.

"The plague! The plague!"

Then, in a moment, anxiety would become panic. Business that had seemed all important that morning would lie forgotten on the desk that afternoon, never to be finished. People seized a few necessities and thronged out along the thoroughfares leading north toward the country, and safety. Up past Canal Street, to tents hastily thrown up in the fields, or to summer homes near Greenwich Village. Anywhere, even to sleep on the bare earth, rather than stay home and face the terrible death.

Marie Bouquement held her needle up to the window and laboriously tried to thread it again. The needle's eye seemed to have grown smaller each time this process was repeated — or perhaps her eyes were no longer as sharp as they had been.

On this hot afternoon she really did not feel like working at all. It had been a week of continuous heat and heaviness, and she felt it more and more with time's passing. But she had been a hard-working woman and the habits of a lifetime were not easily broken. Every day she went out to work, and at home there were services she could render Mr. Nicolas as well as Rosalie and Pierre, for they all continued to live in the Nicolas house. Methodically she took up the white stuff on which she was sewing.

Outside, along Reade Street, the midsummer sun, diffused through the still air like a burning haze, seemed to cast a portentous light over the quite ordinary houses. Marie's African forefathers might have read omens in it, with diviners' accuracy. To her, it was merely oppressive, like the rumor she had heard as she had gone her rounds of the neighborhood—that a man had died suddenly, in the street, of a mysterious disease.

The knock at the door was almost a relief from her own thoughts.

"Oh, Juliette, I'm so glad to see you," Marie said. The young woman was a welcome visitor on any day, but particularly refreshing just now.

Marie led the way back to the sitting room.

"I was just on my way home from market and I thought I would stop in." Marie's sewing caught her quick eye. "Why, Marie, what are you making, a new dress?"

Marie laughed. Juliette always cheered her up. Perhaps

the girl reminded her of her own daughter Adele, lost in the revolt in Saint Domingue.

"Now, Juliette, what would an old woman like me want with a new dress! No, it's a shirt for Pierre. But speaking of dresses —the one you have on is very pretty, and so cool-looking."

"Thank you, Marie." Juliette was pleased. Her disarming smile showed her very even white teeth. "It's new, too. I finished it yesterday—it's made from a new design I have."

"And your kerchief matches perfectly!" Marie exclaimed admiringly. "I always did like the way you tie a Madras kerchief, Juliette. Some day you must show me how it's done."

Juliette lifted her head in a playful pose. It was not the first time someone had asked her for that bit of wisdom. In fact, occasionally some very stylish French lady would ask her the same question. Juliette had a certain flair for such things that others might have envied.

"Oh, I don't know as I should tell you," she answered. "After all, that is my secret, you know!"

Juliette's banter almost dispelled the older woman's mood. But suddenly she heard Pierre coming in, and all her fears rushed back. She went toward the hallway. Surely he would know!

"Pierre! Have you heard anything—they say someone has died of—"

Marie's words fell over each other in her confusion.

Juliette looked up, startled.

"Why, I didn't hear anything in the market just now."

But Pierre's grave face told them the answer.

"It's true," he replied. "I saw them barricading Maiden Lane just now as I passed by."

So it had come again!

The two women studied Pierre's face anxiously. They both knew him so well. They were thinking, Marie and Juliette, of those other times when Pierre had crossed the barriers again and again to go into the condemned houses and tend the abandoned ones struck down with the plague and left alone to die.

Marie was too far advanced in years to feel much terror for herself. But Pierre—he was younger. For he and Juliette, their life still lay ahead. Surely he would not go again this time!

Pierre went on. "When I passed the street, I thought I heard someone cry out from one of the houses behind the barricade. A woman. There was no one else left." And there would be no one. So great was the fear planted in every heart by this dread visitant that human values were lost in panic. Anyone unfortunate enough to lie ill—well, he must endure his throes alone. Unless, of course, one of the city's few doctors had time to find him, or Father William O'Brien, St. Peter's pastor, who had worn himself out year after year in the plague season and once did not go to bed at all for two long months. Unless, of course, Pierre—

Juliette spoke calmly, but her hand shook as she smoothed the patterned skirt of her dress.

"Will you be going back there, Pierre?"

He looked down at her with gratitude. Juliette always understood. She knew he had to go.

"But—" Marie began to protest.

He looked at his aunt almost sternly.

"I feel I must," he explained quietly. "Who else is there?" She could not deny this. Only a supernatural courage enabled a man to meet the plague willingly face to face. And her nephew was one of the few who had this kind of courage. Most people believed black persons were not so susceptible to plague as white persons, but she herself had known of cases among them.

Pierre came over and put his hand on his aunt's shoulder.

"You're a nurse too, Aunt Marie, you see how it is." Marie felt a momentary glow of pride. Yes, that had been her life. And she had taught Pierre much of her own skill. People were always knocking on their door—sometimes in the dead of night—to summon his help at some sickbed. And many a night he spent without sleep in these vigils, without any recompense other than the gratitude of some poor sufferer. They said even his presence made them feel better. He had such a consoling way with him, confident, cheerful, calm. One expressed it more eloquently: "His pity for the suffering partook of Our Saviour's tenderness at the tomb of Lazarus." But the plague, Marie thought, this is something different from an ordinary sickness. Against it one had hardly any chance, for no cure was known and few ever recovered from it. It claimed its victims with terrible speed and violence. Of course people tried to take precautions, but she realized that these were useless if not little more than superstitions: going around wrapped in long shroudlike cloaks sprinkled with vinegar; or firing gunpowder continuously; or practically smothering oneself in every known disinfectant—tar, garlic, niter (potassium nitrate).

Marie shivered despite the heat as she recalled those awful scenes of other years, the hearses rattling up and down the streets day and night, the bells tolling, tolling, hopelessly trying to count the innumerable dead.

Juliette stood up and briskly gathered up her bundles.

"I'd better be getting home right away then," she said firmly. "Will you be leaving again soon, Pierre?"

If she was fearful, her voice hid it. Perhaps she would have gone herself to Maiden Lane if she had just a bit more courage.

Wearily Marie Bouquement went to the hall closet and took out Pierre's little bag of nursing aids and handed it to him. He felt in his pocket to be sure his prayerbook, the one he habitually carried with him, was there. He might need it later on.

Marie knew it was useless to plead with him, so instead she began to pray that the special grace which had protected him so often before might be with him again this time.

Juliette stood waiting.

"I'll walk home with you first," Pierre told her.

As they opened the door a gun barked in the distance. It was the beginning. From now on, until the siege ended, New York would be a city of deserted streets, haunted by the screams of the delirious and all the macabre sounds of death. Many other cities of colonial times shared in this periodic vision of hell, for sanitary conditions were far from advanced. New York's only water system consisted of a small network of pitch-pine timbers laid in 1776, hardly adequate for the normal needs of the fast-growing population. Every morning housewives had to shutter their windows tightly until the procession of slaves to the river bank with their refuse pails was over for the day. Pigs and other domestic animals still roamed the streets freely, eating from gutter-side garbage. And in August, the year's hottest month, the city's one primitive sewer always had to be cleaned. So it was no wonder epidemics came. The plague might be cholera; it might be yellow fever or smallpox. Whatever it was, it was a curse.

Marie began to cry. Suppose, after all, Pierre did not come back!

As he and Juliette went out, Pierre turned to his aunt with a peaceful smile.

"We must take it as God sends it," he said gently.

And so he was to go about in each epidemic, without thought of his own safety, until, many years later, the plagues no longer came.

CHAPTER 13

SOME DREAMS ARE FULFILLED

It was May 21 of the year 1811, and one of Pierre's great dreams had come true.

Rosalie had just gone into the kitchen to begin preparations for supper when her brother came in. Instead of his usual greeting, he came over silently to the table and began to open an envelope he had brought, a look of quiet satisfaction on his face. To him Rosalie would always be his "little" sister. For years he had surrounded her with every protection and solicitude.

Now she looked at the paper Pierre held before her. "Empire Français!" As soon as she saw the heading, she knew what it was—a moment she had looked forward to as long as she could remember. Now that it was here, she did not know what to say.

Rosalie was no longer a slave! The French consul general

said so; Monsieur Nicolas said so. And though she could not make out all the big words in front of her, she knew very well what they meant.

She turned to Pierre, very close to tears.

"Thank you, Pierre. Thank you." She was thinking of all those years when Pierre had faithfully, secretly, saved a little of his pay each week, putting it aside patiently toward the day when he might buy her freedom. It had been an improbable scheme, almost impossible back in the days when he first had envisioned it. He was working for Mr. Merchant then, and his earnings were so small. Later he had given his salary to Madame Bérard, keeping hardly any for himself, but always this little bit was put aside toward Rosalie's ransom. It was a plan very dear to him, to see the sister he loved so deeply made free. Not that he had ever spoken of it. No, never, for it would have been for him much too delicate a subject to discuss with anyone.

Gradually his savings had grown and now the time had come. The odd exchange had been made, so many dollars for so many dreams. Rosalie's freedom was now a legal fact.

Pierre looked down solemnly at the document before them. It meant so much to him. Especially now, since Rosalie's marriage was only a few days off, and her husband-to-be was a freedman.

"It's foolish to cry, isn't it, Pierre?" Rosalie looked up, and tried to smile. "But you know, it makes everything seem so different. Jean and I—" She stopped short as her mind ran on ahead to the future.

"But—" something recalled her to the present, "what about you and Juliette, Pierre? You too are free, and Monsieur Nicolas doesn't really need you now."

Pierre looked thoughtful. It was true. Now he could begin

to think of his own life, something he had always put aside because of the more urgent needs of others. But after all, he was forty-five years old. Juliette and he had waited a long, long time!

"It'll work out, Rosalie," he said reassuringly.

The wedding of Rosalie Jeanne and Jean Noel took place in St. Peter's Church six days later, according to the parish record.

On a warm summer evening a few months afterward, Father Anthony Kohlmann, the Jesuit pastor of St. Peter's Church, sat on a very hard chair before his plain desk in the room that served him as office and reception parlor. It was growing late, and he still had to say his office. He would put things to rights and go upstairs.

The newspapers he had been reading lay open before him, their closely-printed columns crowded with verbose accounts of world happenings. Many of the stories were no more than rumors from incoming ships. Communication was slow and erratic, for the occult language of electric wires had not yet been spoken.

And to Father Kohlmann all those far-off events seemed tonight distant indeed—even inconsequential. In Haiti, Christophe had lost a thousand men in a battle with Pétion. Shadowy warriors in a shadowy land. Or perhaps he was more tired than usual. It had been a very busy day. And one could hardly help, in the quiet of late evening, reflecting on events closer at hand than the unquiet affairs of a tropical island.

The New York *Post,* the strong Federalist paper founded by Alexander Hamilton, discussed little else but the politics of the hour. It was preoccupied with the iniquities of the French and their "plots" against the United States.

More concise, though perhaps hardly more accurate, were the advertisements. Father Kohlmann scanned them with faint amusement. Sometimes they took his mind momentarily off his troubles. Here newly arrived ships carried their cargoes: rum, hemp, and the rest, ready for marketing. A retailer announced some prison handiwork for sale: brooms, stuffers, and paintbrushes. And there were the usual claims for medicinal cure-alls. This time it was Dr. Coitt's Family Pills with their marvelous properties that had been known to work effectively on anything from biliousness to yellow fever. An impressive list of medical men from Vermont attested to their value, and to make it even more convincing, Isaac Tichenor, Vermont's governor, vouched for the honesty of the doctors.

The New York *Herald,* a semi-weekly, spoke discreetly of a newly invented washing machine. Prospective buyers were invited to call at the store to learn—privately, of course— the names of some "respectable persons" who were satisfied customers. And here a noted doctor, Benjamin Rush, praised in glowing terms the benefits of *Chenopodium Anthelmenticum*—Jerusalem Oak.

Jerusalem—the word brought Father Kohlmann back from his mental meanderings. How often had he pictured Christ weeping over this city as he sat in this very chair night after night looking out, in imagination, over his polyglot parish. Pastor of a struggling congregation and vicar general of a bishopless diocese! The burdens of these two posts were enough to discourage any man. But perhaps he wanted to go ahead too fast. He must remember what he had found when he first came to New York in 1808, bringing with him another Jesuit, Father Benedict Fenwick, and four scholastics: a city of about 60,000, a parish of 14,000 souls—chiefly Irish, but French and German as well. It was in that year that New York had been made into a diocese. And in another year, its cathedral was abuilding. He had laid the cornerstone in a rural meadow at Mott and Prince Street, in honor of St. Patrick, and his people's hopes were high. Their bishop was coming!

Months of waiting followed, but the flock still remained shepherdless, except for his own efforts as vicar general. And in Naples their bishop waited, Luke Concanen, O.P. When his passage finally came through, it was not to America, but to eternity.

Meantime, in Rome, in the deep of night, July 5, 1809, Napoleon's emissary Radet had entered the Quirinal, arrested Pius VII who had had the temerity to excommunicate the Emperor, and carried him off to Savona. There in captivity he remained, refusing to name any new prelates until his freedom was restored.

For a time Father Kohlmann must carry on his struggle alone. And a struggle it was to keep some sort of truce between priests and lay trustees, between parishioners of conflicting nationalistic views . . . and always the problem of money.

Weary tonight, he was an easy prey to worry. He must try to direct his thoughts toward the good side of things, where progress was beginning to show. There was the Literary Institute he had founded, a young college, but already beginning to rank with older secular schools. Father Kohlmann was a German and had been a member of the Russian Society of Jesus. Scholarship was dear to him, and in the Literary Institute he had found a means to put his learning to use. For the rest—well, he had determination.

And of course there were some moments when his priesthood meant far more than mediating between opposing factions. Yes, even today he had known, for a little time, the full and fruitful joy of his vocation.

There it was, still before him on the opened page of St. Peter's register. He looked down at that day's entry. Marriages were in the usual order—yet this one, he felt, was not usual. His mind went back to the cool of that morning, and the faces of the man and woman who had knelt before him at the altar. Awesome, they were, the words, the prayers they had uttered together:

> Receive, we beseech Thee, O Lord, the offering made
> for the holy law of marriage; and be Thou ruler of this
> institution of which Thou art Author . . .

Now only the details were before him, remote and formal as he had written them.

August 5, 1811 (Marriage)

> Pierre Toussaint to Mary Rose Juliette.
> Gabriel Nicolas, John Sorbieu, Jerome Willagrand,
> John Benjamin, Donatien Cilardy, Bernard Etienne if
> Others.
> Witnesses who have signed: —

The signatures of Nicolas, Sorbieu, Willagrand were there. Under these, his own name. One thing about these Saint Domingue weddings—there were always a number of witnesses, many more than the required two.

Father Kohlmann closed the book and put it carefully in its place. Tomorrow, he knew, he would see Pierre again at the first Mass at six o'clock, kneeling in the same place he had knelt every morning for over twenty years. This time there would be another beside him.

With the passing of years Pierre had grown more subdued, less exuberant in showing his happiness. Yet what he showed less, he felt more, for he was created to feel intensely—joy and sorrow.

Juliette, years younger, much less burdened with the care of others, still kept her carefree gaiety. They were sharers of a common heritage. For generations their people had survived only because they could laugh and sing and dance forgetfulness to life's cruelty. Juliette possessed that joyous spirit in abundance. It continually delighted Pierre, and amused him too. He humored her little whims like those of a child. But they were one in the spirit of charity.

"I would not exchange my Juliette for all the ladies in the world," Pierre told a French friend. "She is beautiful in my eyes."

They lived on the third floor of the house on Reade Street, the lower part being occupied by Monsieur Nicolas, his cook and Marie Bouquement. Pierre continued to do the marketing for Nicolas, and many other services as well.

It took only a short time for Juliette to turn their two rooms into a very cozy home. She was a born homemaker, an energetic worker, and she could invent beauty in commonplace things—a scarf, a room, the dressing of a dinner table. Entertaining gave her great pleasure, for she loved guests and the company of her friends. People soon discovered the Toussaint hospitality, and returned, time after time, to be warmed by it.

Juliette was also a very good cook. Pierre really appreciated her gift when he came home tired after his day's work and found his dinner waiting. While they were eating, he would talk about places he had visited, persons he had met.

"Oh, today I went again to visit 'Monsieur le Grand,' " Pierre would report. "And what do you think he told me?"

"Monsieur le Grand" was a French gentleman of their acquaintance, a nobleman who had fallen upon very hard times and was trying to keep the wolf from his door in an arrogant, aristocratic, and quite unsuccessful way.

"That he is very wealthy," said Juliette, her eyes flashing merrily.

"Yes, of course, that he is rich, and not only that— "

"He is very well thought of," Juliette added somewhat mischievously.

"That, yes, and more," replied Pierre. "He said to me, 'Toussaint, I have very important friends, you know. They really think very highly of me. Why, every day one of them sends me a nice dinner, cooked by a real French cook.' And then he went on to tell me about everything you've made for him!"

Juliette burst out laughing. For some days she had been preparing dinner for this gentleman and sending it over to him in such a way that he would not know from whence it came.

"He might not have liked it, if he had known," Pierre explained later. "He might have been proud."

The problems of the poor French *émigrés* were very close to Pierre. He could appreciate their plight, for he knew how unprepared they were to earn their living in any of the customary ways. Sometimes his solutions to their financial troubles were quite ingenious.

One French lady confided to him that since her property now provided no income, she was completely without support. He suggested that she begin to teach French.

"But, Toussaint, I could not do that. I know no grammar," she protested.

He thought for a few minutes before speaking.

"Madame, I am no judge, but I have frequently heard it said that you speak unusually pure and correct French."

This was true, for her education in this respect had been of the best.

"But that is a very different thing from teaching a language," she pointed out.

Toussaint spoke slowly, as the idea formed in his mind.

"Would you be willing to give lessons for conversing in French?"

"Oh yes, quite willing."

But he did not leave it at that. At once he began to find some pupils for her among his English friends. Many of them welcomed the opportunity of informal conversational periods for their children, and soon he had a number of pupils for her. She was able to support her family by this simple expedient until rents from her property began to come in again.

In 1812, the year after the marriage of Pierre and Juliette, war between England and America broke out again. The city was in a fever, preparing for the seemingly inevitable attack. When the British burned the White House in Washington, New York was close to panic.

Men and women, and even little children were pressed into service as volunteers to rebuild the old gun emplacements down at the Battery, unused since the Revolution. They dug furiously, even by moonlight, in terror that the city would be shelled. But the expected onslaught never came. English ships blockaded the harbor but there was no attack on the city itself. Shipping came slowly to a halt under the stranglehold of the Embargo and Non-Intercourse Acts enforced against the young republic. Thousands were thrown out of work, and breadlines lengthened day by day.

That was the year of Marie Bouquement's death. She had stayed on in the house with the Toussaints, going out to work by day as long as her strength permitted. She must have been a very old woman. We have the receipt for her burial fee in the handwriting of Joseph Idley, sexton of St. Peter's, in whose loft it is said Mass had been celebrated secretly during the days of the British proscription of Catholic services in New York.

New York, September 1, 1812. The Sum of Fifteen dollars for the Burial fee of Mary Bouquement who was interred in the Catholic ground on the 30 day of August 1812.

The "Catholic ground" was the new cemetery at Prince Street, uptown, where the cathedral of St. Patrick was being built.

After Marie's death Pierre and Juliette went quietly on with their work of helping others. They had begun a custom that would continue for many years: that of taking into their home black boys who had been orphaned or abandoned. Each one would remain for as long as he needed their support, and Pierre saw to it that they learned some useful trade, and he would always find work for them before letting them go.

Their home was frequently a refuge for persons in need. Once they had as guest a poor priest whom Pierre had found alone and destitute in an attic. The man was seriously ill with "ship fever." Pierre brought him home where with Juliette's help he nursed the priest back to health. Similar incidents occurred frequently, and many persons, both white and black, were helped in this way.

CHAPTER 14

A YEAR OF HAPPENINGS

I t was 1815. A year of momentous happenings in New York!

The War of 1812 came to an end. On a February day the sloop *Favorite* came into the harbor bearing the treaty of peace which had been signed with Britain at Ghent almost two months before. The chains of war's anxiety were instantly struck away. According to a contemporary writer and editor, Peter Parley, author of *Peter Parley's Arithmetic*, who was spending that evening at a concert:

> The door was thrown open, in rushed a man breathless
> with excitement. He mounted on a table and swinging a
> white handkerchief aloft cried out: Peace! Peace! Peace!
>
> I ran into the street. Oh what a scene! In a few
> minutes thousands and tens of thousands of people were
> marching about with candles, lamps, and torches, mak-
> ing the jubilant street a gay and gorgeous procession.
> The whole night Broadway sang its song of peace.

And in the same week of February, one of New York's noted citizens, Robert Fulton, died in his home at No. 1 State Street. He was fifty-one years old. It had been seven years since his historic steamboat trip to Albany in thirty-two hours. The city had long since learned how to mourn its great, and when Fulton's funeral cortege started from the Battery up The Broadway, the guns of Castle Garden began to roar, and did not stop until the hearse finally reached Trinity Church. Several learned societies, of which Fulton had been a member, announced a period of mourning, with black crepe to be worn for several months.

There were other, happier events. In the spring, Jean-Louis Lefebvre de Cheverus, bishop of Boston, had made the long journey down the Post Road to dedicate the now completed St. Patrick's Cathedral in Prince Street—then in a field still inhabited by foxes and other wilderness denizens, well outside the city. It was May 4, the feast of the Ascension. A great throng of local residents gathered, out of piety or curiosity, to watch the brilliant ceremonies.

The noted prelate from Boston who was later to be archbishop of Bordeaux and afterward cardinal was famed for his spirit of charity. A refugee from the French Revolution, his arrival in America in 1796 had added brilliance to the flickering lights of American Catholicism. Putting himself at the command of Bishop Carroll, he had asked to be sent wherever the need was greatest, without regard to his own livelihood. Thus he became spiritual father, as well as servant and doctor to the Indians scattered through the vast forests of Maine. Later on, from his shabby cottage adjoining the cathedral in Boston, he had worn away even the stoniest Puritan prejudices by his simplicity and humble service to the poor.

Bishop Cheverus's appearance in miter and flowing cope was an unusual and impressive sight to New Yorkers, unaccustomed to ecclesiastical splendor. Like Solomon entering the temple to prepare it for the glory of the Lord that would come to fill it as a cloud of brightness, he came to bless the new church, built at great expense and effort, a wonder of new world architecture:

> *Terrible is this place; it is the house of God, and the gate of heaven; and shall be called the court of God.*
> *How lovely are thy tabernacles, O Lord of hosts! My soul longeth and fainteth for the courts of the Lord. Amen.*

But months would pass and it would be November of that year before St. Patrick's had its own bishop — the Irish-born Dominican John Connolly, whose arrival from Rome brought to four the number of Catholic priests in New York.

At the end of 1815, in December, Archbishop Carroll would die—John Carroll, first bishop of Baltimore, first diocese of the United States of America. Father Charles D. Ffrench, O.P., came to replace Father Anthony Kohlmann as pastor of St. Peter's Church, Father Kohlmann having been recalled to the faculty of Georgetown University.

Abroad, the fury of the small Corsican had been spent at Waterloo. The peace of Amiens had been signed and England had solicitously provided Napoleon with transportation to St. Helena, a smaller, rockier empire. Pius VII was back at the Vatican and Europe after a turbulent quarter century of war and revolt settled down to a period of painful convalescence.

Pierre's hairdressing work continued to thrive. For Juliette and him, things were going well. There was only one great anxiety: Rosalie. Her marriage had turned out badly. Her husband, in whom she had placed all her hopes for happiness, was a shiftless, irresponsible man. Now after three years of strain and trouble, he had abandoned her altogether. Her health had been declining steadily, and, with a baby on the way, she was a grave concern.

Juliette went often to stay with Rosalie and help her as much as possible during these hard months. But always she would be home again in time to have Pierre's supper ready.

One night, September, 1815, Pierre came home a little earlier and found no one there to greet him. This was most unusual. Stranger still, when he went upstairs, their rooms were empty and no dinner was in sight. It certainly was not like Juliette to go off and forget him.

Instantly he thought of Rosalie. Perhaps she was worse. The house, so still without Juliette's ebullient presence, seemed suddenly dreary. He was sure she was with Rosalie and would go and see.

As he was making ready he heard Juliette coming up the stair. He rushed out into the hallway, searching her face for bad news. She looked worn-out, but she tried to smile as always.

"You have a niece," she told him, slipping off her shawl. "A lovely little girl. Is that not good news?"

"How is she? Rosalie, I mean," Pierre asked anxiously.

Juliette went past him into the room and began to light the lamp.

"Not too well, Pierre. She's weak, of course, because she has been sick so long. But," she struggled to regain her customary optimistic tone, "she will improve with a few days of rest. My mother is with her now. I'm going back later."

"Thank God the child is born," Pierre said. "What is her name?"

"Oh, Rosalie asked me to tell you something. She couldn't talk much, but she wants—she wants you to name the baby."

A strange feeling took hold of Pierre. It was almost as if this were his own child. A strong surge of love for the infant he had not yet seen came over him.

"Euphemia— " he said thoughtfully. "Euphemia is the saint of this day!"

Then began long months of watchfulness and worry. Rosalie's illness dragged on and on. And Euphemia, she was alive—that was all. Both the child and the mother were so weak they lay hesitantly between life and death. Pierre and Juliette kept the vigil, watching, waiting, praying.

And working! For Pierre there would always be work. He had all the customers he could take now, and more waiting. He had a hairdressing shop at 56½ Chapel Street, listed in the city directories of the time, but most of his appointments were kept in the homes of his customers, and this took him daily everywhere through the rapidly-growing city. By now New Yorkers were accustomed to the sound of the jingling bells of the horse-drawn carriages, as they drove up and down the principal streets, but Pierre, being black, was not permitted by law to ride on them.

An exceptionally able walker, he probably did not miss the discomforts of early public transportation. He knew all the streets and all the streets knew him. People saluted him in passing, and going about on foot gave him time for leisurely thought. Tall and dignified he was, always impeccably dressed. He was nearing fifty but he did not show his years. Now and then a wrench of pain—warning of the rheumatism that would plague his latter steps—would come into his knees, but not yet often enough to slow down his pace.

As he went from house to house, he would arrive in the

midst of varying circumstances and would meet many reactions to happiness or sorrow that made a deep impression upon him. One day he came into a house and found it all abustle with the happy preparations for a wedding.

"I well remember," recalled the lady of the house, "the thoughtful manner with which he stood looking about the room."

She asked him the reason for his serious look.

"Oh, Madame," he answered, "I go to a great many places. I go into one house and they cry, cry, cry—somebody dead. I go into another, and it is all laugh, laugh. They are happy and glad. I go to another, it is all shut up dark. They move very softly. They speak in a whisper.

Somebody very sick. I come here, it is all dance and sing, and flowers and wedding dresses. I say nothing. But it makes me think a great deal."

One day he received a somewhat mysterious summons. A boy brought him a note asking him to come to the City Hotel on The Broadway to dress a lady's hair.

He knew the place well. Everybody did, for the City Hotel, recently built on the site of the old Burn's Coffee House, was New York's most fashionable and elaborate place of entertainment. It was famous for its brilliant social events, and people still spoke of the splendid banquet on Christmas Day in 1812, in honor of the naval heroes Decatur, Jones, and Hall, an occasion on which Mayor DeWitt Clinton had presided. And each year Pierre was called upon to coif some of the ladies of his regular clientele for the dances given there by the City Assembly, whose membership included only society's elite.

Pierre walked up Reade Street. It must be some visitor

from another city who had sent for him, he thought. Perhaps even someone from abroad, since the City Hotel was the favorite stopping place of foreign travelers.

He turned south on The Broadway, passing the block- long hospital, and, on his right, the beautiful new City Hall now rising on the outskirts of the city. It had been designed by the architects McComb and Mangin and was being built at a cost of about half a million dollars.

The City Hotel stood next to Trinity churchyard, some distance down The Broadway. At the desk Toussaint presented himself. Did someone there require his services? The clerk of course recognized the noted hairdresser immediately. This way, Pierre was told. The boy would show him to Madame Brochet's room.

Brochet. Brochet. Pierre tried to recall as he followed his guide through the ornate lobby. The name meant nothing. A visitor from France, he guessed. Good! He would be able to speak to her in his own language at any rate. English was still a bit awkward for him. Perhaps this Madame Brochet might bring some interesting news from France.

A middle-aged lady opened the door in answer to the porter's knock.

"The hairdresser you sent for, Madame."

"Oh yes, do come in. How nice of you to come so promptly." She chattered on, delighted at hearing Toussaint's excellent French.

Toussaint took out his large and spotless white apron and began to prepare for the ritual. The maid was busy heating the tongs on a brazier of coals. He laid out the things he would need on the dressing table. It was good, Madame Brochet was saying, to speak one's own language again. It made her feel almost at home, something she had not felt at all since arriving in America.

"I wish I were back in Paris this minute," she complained. "I'm sorry to say I don't find your country so hospitable. Now, in Paris— "

She rambled on. Pierre was used to listening like this. He interrupted only to make certain of how she wanted her hair done. Then he returned to his work, responding only enough to her chatter to be polite.

"Perhaps, Madame, if you were better acquainted here, you wouldn't find our city so unfriendly," he told her. "You know, there are many fine French families here whose company you would enjoy, I'm sure."

"No doubt, Toussaint," replied Madame Brochet. "But after all, one always misses one's own friends. Now, if Mademoiselle Bérard had only been able to come with me — "

Pierre's deft fingers faltered for a moment.

"Bérard?" he repeated slowly. No, it couldn't be! The name of Bérard was a common one in France. "Why Madame, that is a name I know very well. I was—with a family of Bérards in Saint Domingue. But that was very long ago."

"But Aurore—she's from Saint Domingue too. She has often told me about her family's plantation there—the one they used to have, that is. Of course it was lost in the uprising." She paused abruptly. Could it be that this man who was arranging her hair had been one of the slaves who had come to New York with Aurore's brother Jean to escape the trouble?

"This is most surprising, Madame. The family I speak of lived in Saint Marc. They had four daughters—Eulalie, Victoire, Félicité, and De Pointe who was my godmother."

"De Pointe! But that is Aurore. Her father made her change

her name during the Revolution. It sounded too aristocratic, you know. And the other three are her sisters—all married now, and living away from Paris. She hardly ever sees them."

Madame Brochet almost scorched herself in her excitement. Pierre had to snatch the curling tongs away just in time. He too was excited, but he did not want to show it in the presence of a stranger. So many questions came flooding back in that quiet hotel room, so many questions pressed to be asked first.

How strange were the ways of Providence! Had this Madame Brochet traveled three thousand miles, to a country she had not found at all to her liking, only to have her hair dressed by Toussaint so that he might hear again of his childhood playmate and long-lost godmother? Yes, it could be. A chance meeting, apparently. And yet was it?

She told him many things that had happened to the Bérard family, with whom he had lost all touch. Delighted to meet someone who had known her dear Aurore, Madame Brochet talked enthusiastically of her friends. Pierre listened eagerly to each little detail. All came back: persons Pierre had not heard of for decades, memories he had not recalled for years, names he had not spoken for twenty years and more. How were they all? The sons—Lester and Des Glajeux? Lester had died, Madame Brochet told him. But his wife and son were still in Paris, near Aurore. Du Pithon had married an American girl, Mademoiselle Thenet . . .

That night Pierre told the amazing story to Gabriel Nicolas and to Juliette.

"Why not write Mademoiselle Aurore," Juliette suggested. "Madame Brochet would no doubt be happy to take your letter back to Paris with her when she returns."

Pierre sat up late that night working over his letter. After so many years when so much had happened, it was hard to remember all he should say. Most of all, he wanted to assure Aurore of his continued loyalty. Evidently from what Madame Brochet had said she was not too well off. Perhaps there was something he could do to help her, some way to brighten her rather drab existence. He thought again of the little girl for whom he had woven the flower wreaths as they played together in Saint Marc.

Finally he had finished. All that remained was to take the letter to Madame Brochet and ask her kindness in delivering it.

Next day he took it down to the hotel.

"But Madame Brochet isn't here, Toussaint. She has already left," the desk clerk told him.

"But she will be back this evening."

"Oh, no. I mean she has left for France. The ship sailed this morning."

At first it was a sharp disappointment. But he soon realized that Madame Brochet would be sure to tell Aurore of their strange meeting. And Aurore undoubtedly would write. If only he had taken her address from Madame Brochet! But at least he knew she was still living, and perhaps he might expect to hear from her in a few months as mail then traveled.

Juliette was more impatient.

"Now that we know she is in Paris, maybe Mrs. Cruger or Monsieur de Neuville can find her for us."

Catherine Church, their close friend, was now Mrs. Peter Cruger and with her husband often visited Paris where as a girl she had gone to a fashionable convent school, the Abbaye Royale de Panthemont. And the Baron Hyde de Neuville, who with his wife had become so devoted to Pierre when he first came to New York, was now French Ambassador to the United States. Perhaps he could locate Aurore through official channels.

"Let's wait a while and see," Pierre said. He did not want to do anything that would embarrass Aurore, or emphasize her state of reduced fortune.

Three months later the expected message came.

November 27,1815

Madame Brocket on her return to this city fifteen days ago has given me news of you, my dear godson. I as well as my brothers and sisters are truly grateful for the zeal you have shown in wishing to learn something of us and for the attachment you still feel for us all. After the information Madame Brocket gave me, I don't doubt that you will be glad to receive a letter from me. I write to you both with pleasure and I am happy learning that you are prosperous in your affairs and very happy.

As for us, we have never left Paris. Our situation is not a happy one. The revolution deprived us of all our property. My father was one of the victims of that frightful period. After being confined six weeks in prison and under constant inspection of the government on their own place near Paris, both he and my mother died of grief.

My sisters and brothers are married but I am not and am compelled to make efforts to live which have impaired my health which is now very poor. Were it not so, I might be tempted to make the trip you desire, but I am not the less sensible to the offers you have made me through Madame Brocket and I thank you sincerely. It is something for me to know that amidst all my troubles there exists a person who is so much attached to me as you are. I wish I could live in the same town that I

*might give you the details by word of mouth about my
family.*

*Write to me, my dear Toussaint, about your wife.
I know you have no children. Do you know anything
relating to Saint Domingue? What has become of all
our possessions and our former servants? Tell me all you
know about them. Have you any of your former companions in your city? My nurse, Madeline, and your
mother—are they still living? Tell me everything you
know. Adieu, my dear godson. Do not forget to write me
and depend upon the affection of your godmother who
has never forgotten you and who loves you more than
ever since she finds you have always preserved your
attachment to*

Aurore Bérard.

Pierre read the letter to Juliette and Rosalie. It was a sad
letter in a way, yet it was a joy to be in touch with Aurore
again, and already he was beginning to plan little ways to
brighten his godmother's days over which tragic events had
cast so somber a shadow.

"Someday maybe we can all go to Paris to see her," Pierre
told them.

Rosalie smiled wanly. Perhaps—but something told her it
could not be. Tuberculosis daily left her weaker and weaker.
She had been so young when Aurore left Saint Domingue
she probably had no memories at all of her. As she lay in
bed those long hours she sometimes tried to piece together,
from imagination and conversations she had heard, the face
of Aurore in childhood and now as a woman.

Very soon the first gift was on its way to Aurore, who lived
at No. 10, Rue de Tournon, Faubourg Saint-Germain. Juliette
had bought four especially lovely madras handkerchiefs—

something Aurore would surely like as they were said to be the height of fashion in Paris. Juliette was an enthusiastic and shrewd shopper, and as time went on many little parcels containing beautiful presents were carefully wrapped by her capable hands and handed to some trustworthy emissary who on arriving in France would transmit them to Aurore.

From her bed Rosalie tried to share in these little projects, but the year was passing and another spring was to come with no improvement in her condition. Pierre had brought her back to his home when it became certain that she could expect no assistance from her husband. There is a strange silence concerning this man, who had proved such a disappointment to them all. It must have been heartbreaking for Pierre to see his sister at the mercy of so ignominious a character as Jean Noel had proved to be, yet he evidently kept his feelings largely to himself. Whether—as the name might signify— Rosalie's husband was a relative of Juliette's, we do not know, but if so, Pierre's delicacy toward the feelings of others would explain the mystery.

Aurore had soon passed the news of Pierre among the Bérards in and near Paris, and not long afterward a letter arrived from Du Pithon, her brother.

I have read with pleasure and gratitude, my dear Toussaint, all that you have done for my brother and his widow and the attachment you still entertain for our family. Since I have learned all this, I have wished to write you and express the love and esteem I feel for you. It is from Mmes. Delacroix, Riel and Brochet I received these details. I was so young when I left Saint Domingue that I should certainly not recognize your features, but I am sure my heart would acknowledge you at once so much am I touched with your noble conduct.

All my family share these feelings but most particu-
larly my sister Aurore. I do not despair of returning
to Saint Domingue and of finding you there or in the
United States if I take that route.
    Adieu, my dear Toussaint. Give me news of yourself
and believe in my sincere friendship.

Du Pithon

Gabriel Nicolas read the letters from Paris and found in them little cheer. There were too many reminders of days long past, of injustice and upheaval and pain. He was growing increasingly discontented anyway with the passing of years.

The end of the War of 1812 had brought a wave of religious fervor to New York, induced largely by the teachings of John Wesley. Many now frowned upon such amusements as dancing and card playing, and especially upon the theater —chief source of livelihood for a former nobleman turned itinerant musician. Whether this influenced his departure from the city is not certain, for he had never made a very good living anyway, and was always in debt. Pierre often helped him financially, but while this alleviated some of Gabriel's troubles, it only increased his feeling of discouragement.

Leaving New York he wandered southward somewhat indeterminately, stopping here and there to spend some time with other French refugee groups in cities more friendly to the people of the theater. Charleston, Norfolk, and Richmond were places where he found temporary work, and in the summer of 1817 he went farther south to follow a traveling circuit there.

Gabriel wrote Pierre at intervals, always melancholy, always brooding on his inability to return Pierre's favors. His sister Louisa came up from Trinidad and stayed with the Toussaints. Gabriel sent the money for her room and board, but after a time she too became discouraged at her inability to find work, and in a letter her brother asked Pierre to lend her fifty *gourdes* to pay her way to Havana.

From time to time Gabriel was able to pay back small sums of money to Pierre, but he never was able to catch up with all his debts. Nor did he ever return to live in New York again. Pierre made an agreement with Abraham Bloodgood, owner of the Reade Street house, to pay the rent, and assumed all responsibility as the legal tenant there.

CHAPTER 15

ROSALIE'S LEGACY

Pierre had been watching for them, the big man and the small boy, hurrying in the darkness through the rain. He had the door open even before the callers could lift the knocker.

"Come in, Dr. Berger."

"How is she now?"

Pierre took the doctor's dripping coat. The boy, one of those numerous black lads befriended by the Toussaints and given a home with them, ran to get his wet clothes off and climb back into bed.

"Very low, Dr. Berger. It's her breathing—we're worried."

"Let's have a look at her." Dr. Berger took up his bag and stamped up the stairs. Pierre led the way with the lamp.

The baby was in a small room at the end of the hall. He heard the sounds of her tortured breathing even before he saw her lying in the cradle. Her eyes were closed. Her breath labored in harsh, choking gasps.

Juliette sat beside her, rocking her ever so gently.

She stood up immediately.

"It's good of you to come, Doctor. So late at night, and in such a storm."

The big doctor looked down at his tiny patient. Euphemia stirred a little, wrung her tiny hands together briefly, in infant distress.

"Let's see now—she's how old?"

"Seven months, Doctor." Juliette knew the baby still looked almost newborn. At least she had scarcely grown since her birth.

The doctor drew back the blankets. The child was indeed small, hardly a bit of flesh on her. And she seemed to be barely breathing now.

He had seen many other such babies in his long experience —children of tubercular mothers. Mostly there was nothing a doctor could do to save them. Usually they had given up long before this one, the struggle to keep on living just too much for them.

Dr. Berger turned to Juliette.

"I don't like to say this," he told her, gruff and direct as was his way, "but it's just as I told you before—I can't do anything for her. I don't think she'll live—you know that. And maybe, if she didn't, it would be just as well."

Pierre made a quick gesture of protest, but he said nothing. Juliette bent over suddenly and drew the blankets up around the tiny body.

"Perhaps, Doctor," Pierre spoke slowly, deliberately, "there is something more we might do, some remedy we haven't tried."

Dr. Berger closed his bag with an air of finality, the brief examination finished.

"I'm afraid not," he answered. "You've done everything possible to save her. Just go on keeping her warm and raising her head a little so she can breathe better. That's all there is to do. How is her mother tonight?"

Juliette stepped to the door and motioned to a room down the hall.

"In here," she said in a low voice. "I closed the door so Rosalie wouldn't hear the baby."

Dr. Berger followed Juliette into the dark room, his heavy footsteps making loud creaks in the midnight stillness over the uneven boards of the floor.

"Rosalie," Juliette called very softly. "It's Dr. Berger. He wants to see how you are."

She was lighting the oil lamp. The rain hung at the window like a thick black curtain, glistening.

Rosalie awoke and turned to them, her face drawn and hollow after months of sickness. Only her eyes, bright with the brightness of fever, seemed alive.

As usual, Dr. Berger tried to sound cheerful.

"What's this, Rosalie? Still resting in that bed there? I thought you'd be up and about by now."

It was an old joke, one he used almost every time he came, and one that no one could even smile at any more, since they all knew Rosalie would never be up and about again.

"Oh, I don't get any better, Doctor," she said weakly.

"These things take time. Don't forget that, my dear. Now, rest is the all-important medicine for you."

"Why did you come tonight?" she asked suddenly. "Is it— is she worse?" She began to cough, and could say no more.

Juliette came to the bedside.

"Try to sleep now, Rosalie. Everything will be all right. I'll see Dr. Berger to the door."

She led the way out into the corridor again.

"But first, you must have a cup of coffee. To warm you, before going out into the rain again."

Pierre came up carrying the doctor's coat, which he had been trying to dry a little before the fire. Dr. Berger was glad of the steaming hot drink Juliette brought him. These night calls could be bothersome, especially on a stormy one like this. But when the little lad had come banging on his door awhile ago, he knew just what it was. He had come here many nights before, summoned by the same breathless courier to the home of "Uncle Pierre" for the baby Euphemia, or for her ailing mother. Somehow the baby always came through. He couldn't explain how; it wasn't in the medical books. Maybe she would come through this time too.

He did not mind coming, but he couldn't honestly give them any hope. Anyone could see how much the Toussaints had come to love the poor child. He put down the empty cup, said good night briefly, and went out again, back in the downpour to his home, and sleep, his short respite from others' woes.

After he left, the baby suddenly stopped choking and seemed to breathe more naturally.

"See," said Pierre, "she doesn't believe what Dr. Berger said just now."

Euphemia opened her eyes and gazed wonderingly at Pierre and Juliette leaning over her. Then her pathetically tiny face broke into a funny baby smile.

"Oh, look. Look, Pierre. She's smiling. She must be better," Juliette exclaimed.

"Dr. Berger can only go by what he sees. But perhaps God has other plans."

"How can she possibly gain when she can't even eat?"

"Let's try again. You get her a little more milk and I'll sing to her. And maybe, if the rain stops in the morning and the sun is shining, I'll take her out for a walk. It's April, you know. Spring is coming and the fresh air might do wonders for her."

Juliette forgot that she had been up all night. Not only that night, but many nights. She went down to the kitchen and stirred the fire. The windows were beginning to brighten. It would soon be dawn. She opened the door as she waited for the milk to warm; the air outside had changed from chill to a peculiar softness, and the rain had stopped, leaving everything smelling fresh and green. It will be fine today, she thought, as she started back upstairs.

In time, as others reckon it, Pierre was now on the threshold of old age. But in his life, years are counted, not by two's or five's or even decades—but by the score.

There had been twenty years in Saint Domingue. Twenty years watching over his mistress, Marie Bérard. There would be twenty years of letters to Aurore—these were just beginning. And now, after half a century, it was not incongruous to meet him walking down The Broadway on an April morning with a baby muffled in blankets in his arms.

The birds were coming back again to build their nests on the beautiful island of Manhattan. There were as yet no towers of sand or stone waiting to send them hurtling with beaten wings, feathers all awry, to sidewalks far below. Man, it is true, had taken over some of the ground, but not much of it. Gradually his settlement was creeping northward, away from the tip of the island where the North River and the East River met with the sea. But the air still belonged to those created to live in it, and men were still planting trees by the hundreds to beautify their streets, instead of ripping them up by the roots or suffocating them with hard cement.

Especially enticing to the flying homeseekers were the trees of City Hall Park, then on the northern outskirts of the growing city. There they had plenty of choice, the more gregarious birds choosing to build nests in the wide-spreading, hospitable plane trees—those indefatigable hybrids whose vigor still mocks our life-destroying city streets. Some liked the large-leaved branches of the catalpa, its white blossoms exquisitely beautiful in the springtime. Or some, more dignified, picked home sites among the heart-shaped leaves of the poplars, neat and prim, that lined the footwalk round the four-acre park.

People liked the park too, but of course for very different reasons. History had been made there more than once without causing more than a frightened flutter among the branches. Washington had stood there to bid his faithful soldiers farewell after the hard-won campaigns of the Revolution. And in this year, 1817, the park boasted the finished City Hall. Not that the birds ever noticed it, but it was the pride of civic-minded men walking in its shadow.

For Pierre it was the favorite mecca of his outings with Euphemia. At first the baby had lain in his arms, half-sleeping, quite lost in that inarticulate world where to keep on breathing and living was all that mattered. Gradually, as the days grew warmer, Pierre pulled the blankets back just a little, and a little more, and finally removed them altogether as the sun began to shine warmly on the bench where he sat. By that time Euphemia had opened her eyes and seen the green thatchery over her, and felt the sunshine, and breathed the good air with ease. She had heard the birds, and, to Pierre's delight, she began to make little noises that sounded very much like a small bird trying to sing.

It became a pleasant interlude in Pierre's busy schedule

to sit there watching over her and looking out across The Broadway to the famous homes and smart shops that lined it. Houses of the Rutherfords and the Astors. The stores with their gay awnings like bright pavilions all along the street. He could look down Barclay Street, narrow as it was, to where St. Peter's stood. And quite close to him, on what is now the Vesey Street corner, was St. Paul's Chapel.

Euphemia was now two years old—thanks to the good Lord who had given her enough strength to live and grow under Pierre's and Juliette's tender custody—and no longer content to rest in her uncle's arms on these daily excursions. She was really very playful. She held his big firm hand and took a few steps in the grass. She was not sturdy and robust like other children, but tiny and delicate. Even so, she was much stronger than she had been. Pierre watched her face closely, her eyes changing as she reacted swiftly to events around her—the bird flying over her head, or the buttermilk man with his buttermilk cart, bumping over the cobbled street, chanting lustily:

Butter mil-leck! Butter mil-leck!

Or the funny song of the sweeps in the sweep-cart:

Sweep all up from the bottom to the top
Without a ladder or a rope. Sweep oo-oo!

Among the voices of the street callers, whose primitive form of advertising was rich in the lore of New York streets, were mingled the gentler tones of young belles and their swains promenading at midday: a social custom which afforded the benefits of fresh air, a chance to show off one's fine clothes, and, of course, a somewhat stilted conversational exchange with one's companion.

Pierre could see that his little niece had a quick and

observant mind. She watched the carriages rolling by, some with footmen, bearing ladies of delicate complexion (many with coiffures by Pierre) beneath parasols, perhaps en route to the furniture warehouse of Duncan Phyfe, just opposite St. Paul's churchyard, or perhaps to the seed shop of William Cobbett, newly opened in Fulton Street, where rutabagas were selling at a dollar a pound and black pigs went for ten dollars each and were never, of course, purchased by ladies in carriages.

Euphemia never grew tired of watching traffic on the busy street. The boys rolling their hoops with yells of glee. The black-hatted porter trundling his curious one-wheeled barrow, loaded with a passenger's baggage for the ships. And the horse-drawn wagons, with their outsize wheels, awkwardly going their rounds of the city, with drivers hawking their wares—hot corn and potatoes, watermelon and pineapples, Rockaway sand, cattails for bedmaking, rusks for afternoon tea, and "fat salt oysters." The water wagons, with their big barrels lying sidewise, seemed to pass most often. They were filled every day from the Tea-Water Pump on Pearl Street, the city's only source of drinking water, and its center of gossip as well.

Or sometimes he would take her to the Battery for the fresh sea breezes. They would pass along Bowling Green which had just had its name changed from Nobs' Row, or Mushroom Row, and so had gained in dignity. There was a cattle pound there, as well as a very popular promenade.

Euphemia would laugh and clap her hands and try to dance as she had seen her uncle Pierre do. Passersby grew used to seeing them, the gentleman so tall and dignified, and the small girl, so delicate and gay.

She never wanted to go home, but the breeze would begin

to blow cooler, and Pierre had work to be done. A customer waiting, or some act of kindness. So he would pick her up once more, as he had done countless times, and carry her along the street, singing a gay old Creole air that had first been sung in the slave huts of Haiti. It was the music of a dark mother crooning over a dark child and it must have sounded strange in the city.

When they came to the comer of Barclay Street, they would stop at St. Peter's for a brief visit. Euphemia now seemed to know they would always stop there on the way home. And then they would go north on Church Street to Robinson, Warren, and Chambers. Finally to Reade Street, where Juliette was waiting. Many, many steps. But Pierre hardly noticed the child's weight. He was very strong and she was very light.

One spring afternoon in 1817 Euphemia had fallen asleep in Pierre's arms, made drowsy by the singing and the sun and the rhythm of his walking. He looked down on her with inexpressible love, for today she had seemed to be his in a very special way.

Rosalie's long trial had just ended. Pierre's grief over his sister's death was made more poignant by the presence of her child. Yet he realized that his loss could not be compared to Euphemia's, and he determined that they would make it up to her as well as they could, he and Juliette.

There she was now, waiting for them in the doorway. Juliette was such a warm and loving woman. Perhaps she had wondered sometimes why God had never given her a child of her own. Now she could see a reason. He might have been thinking of this little one who needed mothering so much that her very life from day to day seemed to depend on it.

Aurore Bérard seemed to understand well how they

felt, when she wrote Pierre, some months afterward, about Rosalie's death:

> *The loss you have endured of your sister — my sor-row — these are true sufferings. In serving as the father of her child you will pay tribute to your loss and your heart will be content. I pray that she will respond to your care and will be grateful to you for it.*

CHAPTER 16

COUNSELOR AND FRIEND

After fifty years or so, a man is bound to be known for what he is. Pierre had been a man of action, not one to speak much for himself, but others were not so reticent. The stories were beginning now to gather in about him, even as the years, like a cloud, imperceptible, yet luminous, shadowy yet obscuring nothing.

The poor and the sick came to him for physical, material help and encouragement. Their testimony to his charity is implicit in those little tortuous, staccato, humiliated notes they sent him.

Those well provided with the world's goods came to him for something more subtle—understanding. It was, according to those who knew him best, his greatest gift. Some of these people were more articulate, given to writing letters and keeping voluminous journals. In the fine houses of the town a legend of Pierre was beginning.

Pierre, of course, did not hear it, this tide rising secretly from the springs of his own remarkable goodness. As he went his daily rounds, he heard his own footsteps, the blending of the street noises with his own meditations.

"Good-by, Uncle. Come home early today so you can come to my doll party."

The parting words of little Euphemia still echoed in his ears, as she had stood in the doorway a few minutes before. Her small white apron exactly matched Juliette's. Probably right now the two of them were already beginning to set out the ingredients for tonight's gumbo.

He drew his appointment slips for the day from his pocket. First he must go to Mrs. Peter Cruger's very early for this was her "at home" day and a busy one in her household. She was one of his best customers. For one thing, her fine hair and distinguished face showed off his handiwork to perfection. Over the years he had also learned to look upon her as a true friend.

After that, he was due at the Hamiltons'. No doubt Eliza's hair needed cutting again That was a bright little girl—Eliza. She loved to hear his stories and would laugh merrily at his jokes. Sometimes her high spirits caused trouble—she could be very naughty—and then he had to be a bit stern and remind her to obey her father James Hamilton, the third son of the brilliant statesman. Pierre must not forget to ask him today for his regular contribution for the orphans' fund. He was one of the few men whose name appeared on the printed lists of subscribers to the Ladies' Auxiliary of the Catholic orphanage.

Sometime during the afternoon, perhaps on the way home, he would drop in for a visit with Mrs. Schuyler on Canal Street. That was something he never failed to do each day. He knew many members of the illustrious Schuyler family, but she had a special place. Outside of his family, she would always be his closest friend. Mary Anne Sawyer she had been, from Newburyport, Massachusetts, and she had become the second wife of Philip J. Schuyler, son of the famous General Schuyler of Saratoga and Albany. Mrs. Schuyler found herself turning to Pierre for companionship more and more. She leaned on his courage and acted on his counsel.

Pierre was a familiar, even indispensable, member of many households. Everyone, from kitchen servant to master of the house, was quite likely to consult him on widely varied problems. In one letter, a friend asks him if he should remarry, saying that Pierre was the only one he would think of consulting.

Into each house he brought a genuine concern for everyone in it, and he never left without making that concern felt by all. But it was the women, those whose hair he might dress daily for many years, who placed their whole confidence in him. They always looked forward to his visits with keen expectation.

As one of them put it, "Some of the pleasantest hours I pass are in conversation with Toussaint, while he is dressing my hair. I anticipate it as a daily recreation."

He always looked so dignified, and spoke so courteously. Something about him commanded confidence. You could say anything that came to mind, without fear of betrayal. Rare intuition, rare tact, and the rare ability to put an anxious mind at ease. Was this Pierre, the hairdresser? Behind the apron, the polite exterior, was a man who possessed not merely judgment and wisdom, but true compassion.

A strange situation had been created. He was going to them as a humble tradesman, doing his work well, and thereby earning his livelihood. But they were receiving him as a friend and advisor more trusted than any in their social circles.

He had a great sense of the fitness of things. In fact, on occasion, it was up to him to set the keynote of the conversation. Sometimes the ladies liked to gossip. Naturally Toussaint knew everything. As he went from house to house gathering confidences, he could not help becoming acquainted with the skeletons abiding in all the closets. But one could not pry the least little bit of information about one's neighbors from him. Sometimes it was too tantalizing.

"Do tell me, Toussaint. . . " The lady looked earnestly into her mirror, the face of curiosity looked back, and above that, the pleasant impassive brow of Pierre. "Come now, I'm sure you must know about it."

He was always polite.

"Madame, Toussaint dresses hair. He is not a news journal."

The face in the mirror changed, became slightly pink and abashed.

"Oh—oh, yes, of course!" One could never get anywhere with him!

Society had its unwritten laws. When these were violated tempers would flare. The face in the mirror would be indignant, the eyes sending out shafts of genteel lightning.

"Tell her, for me, when you go there— "

And Pierre would calmly set another ridge of hair.

"But I have no memory," he apologized.

Madame would cease to fume and settle back uneasily in her straight chair. Everyone knew Toussaint's memory was better than most. They had all heard him quoting from his favorite authors, Bossuet and Massillon, page after page at a stretch. It was no use!

He knew the time for speaking, and the time for silence.

Sometimes they played on his sense of humor. Mrs. Stevens liked to do this. The wife of John C. Stevens, son of the John Stevens who had first applied the principle of steam propulsion to boats, Maria Stevens belonged to a distinguished family of inventors and sportsmen.

"I am told the town is very gay," she wrote him once from her winter retreat in Annandale, "nothing but balls and parties, every one better than the next. As for you, what do you think? I hope you answer my letter to tell me all the news, all the fashions, all the *scandals,* all the rumors, in fact everything that has happened since I left town, good and bad."

It must have been written with a smile for she well knew what manner of "scandal" she would ever learn through Pierre. But she could joke about it, for she was always *au courant* with social events. When it came to entertaining, no one outdid her. Her balls were dazzling. She always had the "right" people.

At times her invitations were issued in a somewhat curious manner. She would drive ceremoniously in her carriage to Grace Church, halting just long enough to pick up its sexton, Mr. Brown. For some obscure reason, Mr. Brown was a living directory of fashionable addresses and when he went along, she was sure of leaving her coveted bids at all the proper places. Each year, on New Year's Day, she would punctually pause at Pierre's door in Reade Street and leave her gift, with a little note of affectionate good wishes.

There were many like her among Pierre's customer-friends. His appointment lists read like a register of New York's great names: LaFarge, Binsse, Cruger, Hamilton, Schuyler, Hosack, Livingston, and many more.

At every house where there were children, he was invariably

greeted by them as soon as he entered the door. He always had stories to tell them, droll or serious, and if he put in a word of sober advice now and then it was done so deftly they never suspected the "moral" of the fable.

"Dance for us, Toussaint," they would clamor. And setting down his hairdressing kit he would do a few graceful turns for them. Tall and supple, he seemed to dance as easily as others walked. Sometimes he would bow low, saying,

"And this, young ladies, is how your dear mother used to dance, when she was a young girl."

"Long ago?"

"Long ago!" and he would smile at their childish grasp of time as he demonstrated with consummate dignity the complicated ballroom patterns of other years.

One of them folded away and kept a little slip of paper on which Toussaint had written out painstakingly the routine of a dance he knew:

> En avant 4 et en arrière, ir chassés & dechassée sans
> rigidon / balancés vos Dames à vos place & un tour de
> main. . . .

Back on the plantation in Saint Marc, when Pierre was a boy, he had often made the Bérards laugh with his clever imitations. Later he realized this gift of his could be a cruel weapon, used by an acute observer of human foibles to bring pain to its victims. He resolved to give it up. But he could never give up his flair for entertaining, his wonderful sense of humor, his gay spirits. Sometimes he played the violin for small parties and had even taught a few of the boys who stayed with him to play it, just as a pastime.

He was always called upon when the time came for haircuts for the young people. Sometimes several children would be gathered together in one place, as at the Binsses', where there was a small school.

> *Mes demoiselles Hayward, Cruger, Yates, Battelle,*
> *Scarborough, Hosack, Sanford, Packard, Hamilton,*
> *d'Wolf, Jackson, Irving and Drake prient Toussaint*
> *d'avoir la bonté de venir de bonne heure.*
>
> Madame Binsse

He would certainly have had to go *"de bonne heure,"* early, to take care of so many. Very often his help was asked in the exciting preparations for an important debut.

> *Mrs. S. Jones will thank Toussaint to call tomorrow if he*
> *is disengaged, to cut the children's hair. She also wishes*
> *Toussaint to dress her son Monday evening for the Ball*
> *. . .*

One of his favorites among the young people was William Schuyler, Mary Anne's stepson. Pierre wrote William while he was away at school in Massachusetts.

> *I assure you indeed that I am proud to receive a letter*
> *from Monsieur William Schuyler for I think and I am*
> *certain that you have the sensibilities of a true nobleman,*
> *that is to say, un homme comme il faut, so much so that*
> *should you ever marry, and I should have the happiness*
> *to receive a letter from your lady, I should consider her*
> *the Comtesse William Schuyler. . . . I go every day to see*
> *Madame, your mother. She is very well and your cousins*
> *are always in good spirits. The young ladies hope to see*
> *you this Winter at Mr. Bancel's ball. . . .*

His gentle humor won the hearts of the young. They were never afraid to express their thoughts to him quite openly. Once a little girl confronted him with a serious question:

"Toussaint, do you live in a black house?"

He could laugh at that, afterward, for he was never self-conscious about the fact that he was black.

What he said to the child might have been, "Yes, in a way — "

Nowadays all the little ones reminded him of Euphemia. She was five years old, and very much the center of his many-sided life. Everyone said she was an unusually engaging child. She had a way with her, strikingly gentle, amusingly quaint. If ever a child were guarded lovingly from life's rough and tumble, Euphemia was. Now that her health was no longer a critical issue, Pierre and Juliette were concerned about her education.

Always uppermost in their minds was the cultivation of their foster child's spiritual qualities. With the delicacy of an expert teacher, Pierre inculcated little lessons of love and kindness. He must have known that by the age of five, character is already well formed. He felt poignantly the trust placed in him by Divine Providence in leaving her to his care. And that care was always tenderness itself, but never mere softness, for he had known the use of discipline in his own life.

Many little gifts and tokens of affection came to her from Pierre's friends, whose attitude toward Euphemia was an overflow of his own solicitude. She was literally surrounded by love. Juliette could not have cared more for a daughter of her own. And Pierre would introduce her proudly to his friends, putting his arm around the child's frail shoulders, as "my Euphemia."

Even on his busiest days, he would often be thinking of her, things to do for her, plans for her pleasure or profit.

Always he looked forward to the evening homecoming, for no matter how tired he felt, he would forget all about that when he saw Juliette and Euphemia at the door to greet him.

Each day as he turned the corner into Reade Street, an ordinary street of ordinary frame houses, he knew Euphemia would be waiting to be swung up in his arms. Still small and delicate, she went up in the air as light as a song, despite his weariness.

"Carry me, Uncle. A little ride, please." She held on tightly till he rode her around the house. Then she let him sit down and listen to her little stories of the day's happenings. Juliette, good housekeeper that she was, was initiating their small niece into all the secrets of the domestic craft, so one day Euphemia had several things to report.

"Aunt Juliette let me help her with the soup today, and we wrapped up a package to send to Mademoiselle Aurore."

But she was saving the most important thing for the last. "Oh, Uncle, I nearly forgot. I have a s'prise for you. Hide your eyes. Don't look now, till I tell you to."

She flew out of the room. A moment later she was back, walking ever so slowly, balancing his customary cup of coffee with tremendous concentration as she carried it toward him.

"Look, Uncle, your coffee. This time I made it all myself!"

CHAPTER 17

FRANCE OR AMERICA?

In thirty years, Pierre's footsteps had made a well-worn path to St. Peter's Church in Barclay Street. It was not a long walk from Reade Street, only five or six blocks, but each morning as he started out very early and passed along Church Street in front of spacious tree-surrounded Columbia College, he was deepening a habit which gave direction to his life.

Here he was again, the solitary black man, who daily passed that way with his long and vigorous step. Today the sharp chill made him shiver and walk more briskly as he went home from the six o'clock Mass. There was no sun yet, only the thin, still light of a winter dawn.

Others might need a whole wide world for the projection of their life portrait. Pierre had chosen to make this handful of city blocks enough. Like a Japanese painter who with infinite patience adds thousands of tiny brushstrokes to bring out bit by bit the exquisite perfection of some miniature scene, Pierre was gradually forming himself by means of many subtle lines and shadings—acts of kindness and self-forgetfulness, piety, faith. All ornaments on a canvas basically spiritual.

But today his thoughts were far away. In different circumstances Pierre might have been a traveler. Beneath his habitual self-discipline was a restlessness, born perhaps of the fact that he was, in a sense, always an exile. New York had given him a place, even a place of distinction, but his roots could never be put down there.

Son of an uprooted people, his life had touched three continents. Africa—the half-forgotten lore of an enslaved people stretching back into hidden forests. Europe—for the colony of Saint Domingue had been thoroughly French in culture. And now America, a hard new language, a land almost too young for legends.

Only three blocks to the west of his hairdressing shop lay the broad Hudson, avenue of world adventurers. He had often walked along the harbor, the bowsprits of clipper ships shadowing his head and nudging the staid windows of the countinghouses on the inland side of the street. There one could smell the exotic fragrances of cargoes from far-off lands: spices and perfumes, tar and turpentine. Sometimes they brought back memories of his one long voyage, and tempted him to look beyond his familiar streets and walks.

But his sense of responsibility had always been too strong to allow these fanciful journeys too firm a hold. He was a man, above all, who would always be found where his obligations lay. But today, as he hurried toward Reade Street after Mass, a new aspect of the question occupied his mind. Was it not possible now that his duty lay abroad, in France, where Aurore Bérard was? Surely she needed his help, for her letters were full of sorrow, hardship and loneliness. From here, there was so little he could do. Letters and gifts. And asking all his friends to visit her when they went to Paris. Not much, certainly. Perhaps he should go there to live, or perhaps—but he would talk it over with Juliette first.

She stood up from the fireplace, poker in hand, as he came in.

"It just won't come up! Such a cold day, and I can't get it to burn."

She gave the offending logs another poke, as if to leave no doubt of her resolve that they must do better.

"Here, you try, Pierre. I'll bring in your breakfast."

Pierre laid aside his coat. The morning chill had not left the room. He bent down and coaxed the fire gently, easing the charred wood over into the hesitant flames.

Juliette soon bustled back into the room.

"Anyhow, the coffee's hot. Oh, and here's a letter. A boy brought it yesterday but I forgot to give it to you last night."

Pierre sat down and glanced at the folded paper. The precise writing told him who the writer was: Jean Sorbieu. That same script had appeared in the record of Pierre's and Juliette's wedding, and on his freedom papers, both of which his friend Sorbieu had legally witnessed.

With the end of the Napoleonic Wars a slow trickle of refugees began returning to France. Many hoped to be indemnified for their war losses by the new government. Others were merely homesick for the life they had always known. Sorbieu was one of these. A former planter of Saint Domingue, he had been dissatisfied with life in America and, with his family, had gone to live in Rouen.

Even before opening the letter, Pierre knew what it would be, for Jean's letters, and there were many of them, never varied greatly. He was a critic, and rather a sharp one, of

American ways, especially in ecclesiastical matters.

As a parishioner of St. Peter's, Sorbieu, like many of the French in New York, had taken a deep and personal interest in church affairs. This was to be expected, for back in 1785 the city's first Catholic church had been incorporated under the leadership of the French consul, Hector St. Jean de Crevecoeur, and a small group of twenty-three Catholics. The difficulties of those early years had been numerous. It was not only the financial burden that must be borne by New York's handful of Catholics, but those most zealous for the church's welfare did not, unfortunately, always agree on what was best for her.

Pierre had listened by the hour to Sorbieu's views on these matters and now his letters were just a continuation of the same endless discussions.

Juliette brought her cup of coffee to the table and sat down to listen as Pierre read aloud the fine and crowded script.

> *I am indeed sorry that the clergy of New York don't agree better and that the practice of Religion is made a source of suffering. It would be well if they knew of the pomp and magnificence with which Divine service is celebrated in France in all the Churches. This thought would remove perhaps the apathy in which I find all Irish priests particularly who because of a Protestant environment are always lax in divine worship.*
>
> *Formerly there were about thirty parishes at Rouen, which are now reduced to twelve ... in each of these churches every morning there are prayers, sermons, Mass, and Benediction after Mass, evening prayer, sermon and le salut which is never omitted. Compare this then with New York and judge the difference. . . .*

*I fear indeed that Saint Peter's won't return to its
former state, but since we can do nothing about it let
us be content to do our duty and to take advantage of
the means we have to obtain our own salvation. I wish
that the same means existed in America as in France for
everyone to profit from.*

He was referring to the controversies which were going on
among the clergy and people of New York, mainly between
those of French and Irish origin. Sorbieu had been a supporter
of Father Peter Malou, who spoke only French and had
become the confidant of the French Catholics in New York.
Whatever the issues involved in these dissensions, their chief
origin appeared to be nationalistic rather than religious.

Anyhow Pierre remained aloof from all such quarrels.
Although his background certainly should have led him
to favor the French views, he preferred to be merely a
loyal parishioner, supporting his Church through all
her vicissitudes and not questioning the decisions of the
authorities.

"Going abroad hasn't changed Monsieur Sorbieu's
disposition," Juliette exclaimed wryly as Pierre finished
reading. "He's still complaining about things, just as he used
to over here."

Pierre folded up the letter thoughtfully.

"He is good, but discontent is natural to him. He wants
nothing less than perfection."

"I thought once he was back in France he'd be happy!" A
melancholy temperament was hard for Juliette to understand.

"Such a man will never be truly happy. But there is some
truth in all he says," Pierre gently defended his friend.

Juliette spoke up suddenly.

"Do you think things are really so much better over there?"

"It must be so," Pierre answered. "Everyone says the same thing. Madame Larue's letters are much the same as Jean's, as far as that goes."

"In that case, let's go there ourselves." Juliette was often known to speak first of what was in his mind. He glanced up quickly, but her eyes showed she had not meant it seriously.

"Would you really like to go to France, Juliette?"

"You mean for good, Pierre? But business is so good for you here in New York!"

"Business, yes. But Mademoiselle Aurore—she is sad, lonely. There's little we can do for her when we are so far away."

Juliette was always practical. "But what could we do for her over there if you had no income? She says she is not well off either!"

Then she added, more gently, "But maybe you are right. If you think it's best, then let's go over and be with her. But first, shouldn't we ask Mademoiselle Aurore what she thinks of the idea?"

"I'll write to her tonight," Pierre agreed.

Euphemia, who had wakened and come downstairs, heard what they were saying from the doorway. She came quickly up to the table and climbed on her uncle's knee.

"Are you going away to France, Uncle?" Two small lines of worry appeared between her eyes.

"Not without you, little one. Of course, not without you."

"Oh!" The anxiety left her. She smiled happily.

"Then I could play with Eugene and Caroline, couldn't I, over there?" They were Sorbieu's children. She ran over to her doll house near the hearth and began rearranging the tiny furniture.

Pierre and Juliette needed no more than that moment to notice her eagerness—a child's innocent anticipation of the exciting unknown. It lighted up her delicate little face, still marked with the frailty no tender care of theirs had ever quite erased.

Ocean voyages could be harrowing for the strongest men. Weeks spent in crowded, dirty cabins. Never enough food, or enough really good food. It would hardly be right for the child.

Juliette went abruptly to stir up the fire and button the child's warm wrapper firmly around her thin shoulders.

"Uncle, when you go to Mrs. Tessandie's, would you ask her to make some candles for my baby house? I need new ones now." Euphemia was busy fitting a small taper into a toy candlestick, all thoughts of foreign travel quite forgotten.

"We'll see, Euphemia," Pierre promised.

Juliette was clearing the table.

"Will you be passing Madame Gravier's today?" she asked.

"I can go there this afternoon. Is the package for Mademoiselle Aurore ready? I think Madame Gravier sails for France at the end of the week."

"Yes, it's here, all wrapped. I do hope she likes the color of the crepe de Chine. It will make a lovely dress." Juliette could see in her imagination how it would look when it had been made up. She and Pierre always put the greatest care into their selection of gifts for his godmother. Sometimes Aurore even demurred a little in thanking them, wondering whether they had not gone to too great an expense for her.

It was time now for Pierre to go to work. He went over his day's schedule mentally. It was "First Monday" again, and Sister Cecilia up at the orphan asylum would be looking for the money he had collected for her during this month.

One of his customers, Madame Larue, had been an active supporter of New York's Catholic orphanage since its door first opened in 1817. As a member of the Ladies' Auxiliary she had collected contributions regularly from various acquaintances and handed them in to the Sisters of Charity on the appointed days.

Pierre, because his work caused him to make the rounds of many houses, had always helped her take up these collections. When she went abroad to live, he had taken over the work entirely. Even now, whenever she wrote, she was sure to remind him of her orphans, and to beg him never to abandon his concern for them. She still faithfully sent him her own donation, all the way from Le Havre.

He took out the envelope with the money in it, to make sure the list was all complete. With his customary neatness and accuracy he had written the names of all the subscribers, with their addresses, and the amount each one had given, sums as a rule ranging from one to five dollars.

"How much can you give Sister Cecilia this time, Pierre?"

"A bit more than usual—$53.50."

Juliette, who knew her prices well, was calculating just what that amount would buy—how many pairs of small shoes, for instance?

"Madame Larue will be happy about that. We must write and tell her how well the collections are coming."

"Yes," Pierre answered, "the good people I visit are very generous to the children. But more than anything they need a new home just now, one large enough to take care of them all."

"Won't that come soon, Pierre? I know Father Power works hard trying to raise money for the building."

Pierre shook his head. "He knows how badly it's needed.

But it will take much more time— ”

Euphemia looked up suddenly.

“Uncle, won't you take me to the orphanage sometime with you, to visit the children?”

“Some day I will, Euphemia, but Prince Street is too far for you to walk just now.”

“Then bring them all back with you. Aunt Juliette can give them tea and I'll let them play with my dolls.”

Pierre smiled. His niece's generous impulse pleased him.

He put on his coat to leave. Perhaps, after all, his place was right here. Euphemia might never be very strong. And the Sisters of Charity, Mother Seton's daughters, had come to depend on him a great deal.

The question of going to France did not trouble him seriously again. Soon afterwards two letters from abroad confirmed his own views.

> *Madame Cruger thinks as I do [Madame Larue wrote], in your regard. It would be much better for you to remain in New York than to come to France. You are loved and known, and without flattering you, are well-thought of by all upright people. Here it would take some time to acquire the good reputation that means so much in life. There is very little hairdressing here except by maids who all know how to arrange hair. It is only on great occasions that a coiffeur is needed. . . .*

Aurore also discouraged his coming, but with regret.

> *I have seen Mr. Sorbieu today. This gentleman appears to be much attached to you which gives me great happiness. We talked together of your wish to come to France. If I consulted only my own desire to see you, I*

should say, come at once. But your happiness, my dear godson, is what I think of above all things and since everyone from New York tells me that you are happy, highly esteemed and much beloved, by most respectable persons there, would you be so well off here?

Those who know your resources better than I do may advise you with more confidence. If I were rich, it would be of little consequence. I would call you near to me, for I should be too happy to know a person to whom I could give all my confidence and of whose attachment I would feel certain.

But my position is a sad one. I could not be useful to you and I fear that you would not be as happy as you deserve...

Her letters were infrequent, because it was hard for her to find someone to deliver them for her. Few of her friends ever came to New York, and she was not close to any port where outgoing ships might take them aboard.

Sometimes she worried about Pierre, fearing that some people might take advantage of his goodness. When she heard, in a roundabout way, that he was still supporting some of the old slaves from the Bérard plantation, she warned him against encouraging laziness in those who were able to work.

All her letters, gentle, affectionate, noble in spirit, showed deep concern for Pierre's happiness. She would counsel him over and over to remain always loyal to the Faith he had received as an infant under her sponsorship.

But Pierre scarcely needed such advice.

Storms, rivalries and financial crises might hover over St. Peter's, but the little gold cross on her spire remained steadfast. And Pierre too was steadfast, another kind of beacon to guide uncertain souls.

CHAPTER 18

EUPHEMIA

Juliette smoothed the heavy white damask cloth over the edge of the table, briskly adjusting it here and there till it fell evenly in soft billows. Then she bustled about, setting out the cups and saucers of her prettiest china.

"Bring me the napkins, Euphemia, please," she called out. Euphemia was taking them from the drawer of the chest, where they lay on top of layers of neatly ironed linens.

"Aunt Juliette?" There was a question on Euphemia's mind that had been bothering her all day. But they had been so busy preparing for the guests, she did not like to interrupt.

"What is it, dear?" Juliette was thinking about the tea party she was giving that afternoon. "Did you get out the best napkins?"

"Yes, Aunt, here they are." Euphemia set them in place on the table. All that morning she had been helping her aunt, polishing the silver tea set, and all the other dishes and silver pieces, many of them gifts from friends abroad. Euphemia always liked days like this, when everything was a happy flurry of excitement and the house looked especially nice.

Everyone said Aunt Juliette was a wonderful hostess. And she must be, because so many people were always coming to call. Juliette would sit at the head of the table, pouring her delicious French chocolate. And Euphemia, eight years old now, was allowed to pass the little iced cakes Uncle Pierre always brought from the bakery when company was expected.

"I've been wondering, Aunt Juliette," Euphemia began again. "I know Miss Meetz is coming today, and—oh, I do wish Uncle would let me take music lessons from her. She told me she wants to teach me."

"Yes, that's right, dear. She would like to give you lessons." Juliette knew how much it meant to her niece, who loved music and had a beautiful voice. "But your uncle must decide that. Here he comes now. Run out to the kitchen, will you, and bring in the teaspoons and that sugar bowl we polished."

Euphemia skipped out, and Juliette paused in her work to look after the small graceful figure in the doorway. The child was so good and always quick to obey. Juliette hoped that Pierre would say yes to the music lessons today.

After the refreshments Euphemia went out to play, and Juliette took her guests into the cheerful little parlor, where Pierre joined them. Their hospitality was praised by all who ever went there, and often there were numerous white persons among their guests.

"Have you and Juliette thought over my suggestion of giving Euphemia music lessons?" Césarine Meetz, whose mother had been Pierre's customer, hoped to have the matter settled today. She was eager to begin Euphemia's instruction.

"It's very kind of you, Césarine," said Pierre, "but I don't know whether it is a good plan."

He thought it might be a waste of time and money. Also, he did not want to put ideas into the child's head. Pierre would have preferred that she be a loving child of God, sensitive to His Will, rather than a person of merely intellectual or artistic attainments.

"But I know Euphemia is really gifted." Césarine pressed her case gently, for she loved the little girl very much. She was only sixteen herself, but already an accomplished musician. "She has a lovely singing voice, you know."

Pierre could hardly be deaf to praises for his Euphemia. Besides, he loved music himself.

"I know," he smiled, "she sings like the birds, and they haven't been taught!"

Césarine laughingly pointed out that Euphemia was no bird, though indeed she was graceful enough to be one, and she could benefit from some training. It might even be valuable should she have to support herself later on in life.

This was a strong argument, but Pierre had another objection.

"How could she come to your house for the lessons? We never allow her to go out alone."

"Oh, that's easy," replied Césarine. "I'll come here. Two or three times a week. I'd love to do it. She'll be a fine singer some day, wait and see."

"No, that would be an imposition," Pierre protested.

"I'll bring her to you, then," Juliette offered.

Pierre paused thoughtfully. He knew Juliette was in favor of the plan.

Césarine saw that she had won.

"Oh, good," she exclaimed. "It's all settled then. We can start right away, this week. Would you like to hear the new song I've just learned?"

Once the lessons began Pierre was deeply interested in Euphemia's musical progress. After much consideration, he even bought her a piano, so she could practice at home, and play for them. Juliette faithfully took her to Miss Meetz' three times a week, and just as Césarine had predicted, Euphemia showed a great aptitude for music and advanced very rapidly.

Her eighth birthday had gone by. It was 1823 and Pierre had told her his new plan. After this, every Friday was to be letter-day in the Toussaint household. Euphemia, as an object lesson in composition, was to write her uncle two letters a week, one in English, one in French.

She bit the end of her pencil and tried to think what to say this time. The paper before her seemed to grow bigger and blanker and very white.

Suddenly an idea popped into her head. Nursery rhymes! She knew them all. She would write one out for Uncle Pierre, and that would be her letter. She bent over and wrote laboriously, trying to form the letters clearly as she had been taught. It was really hard work, this letter writing, though Uncle Pierre certainly did not seem to think so. He wrote letters all the time, and always seemed to know what should go next.

Hickory, dickory dock, the mouse ran up the clock—

After four lines, both rhyme and letter came to an abrupt end. "Adieu, dear uncle," she knew that was the way to end, and then her name, hurriedly, for she heard Mrs. Ruckel coming down the hall. Her letter must pass her English teacher's scrutiny before being handed to Pierre. And Mrs. Ruckel was very particular about such things. She had rented a room in their house, and gave English lessons there, not only to Euphemia, but to her other pupils as well. It was like having a school in one's own home, a little one, just as the Bancels had their big one.

That first year of letter writing, Pierre would have many of these little nursery rhyme notes. Or sometimes, with a greater effort, she would write out a poem he had taught her. Once it was all ten verses of "Hark the Herald Angels Sing." Another time, his favorite hymn to the Blessed Mother, "The One Thing Needful." He must have smiled, reading them. At least the child had a good memory.

By the time she was nine she could tell him little stories, usually with pointed morals, or pass on some current bit of news heard from her elders. Only two or three sentences at most, but a picture of what a small girl in those days thought about. Sometimes she was thinking about nothing. Then she would apologize. "Dear Uncle, I have no head for composing," or "I forgot it was Friday," but she always promised to do much better next time.

Euphemia's written French was not very fluent, though she probably spoke it well. But Pierre wanted her to become proficient in his native language and when she was twelve she would have a French tutor.

There are in existence over four hundred letters from Euphemia to Pierre. Hundreds of Fridays, and a small serious old-fashioned child recording her impressions of life around her and her own old-young thoughts. From her protected nest in Pierre's home she looked out candidly at the world, the New York of her day, reporting with disarming ingenuousness and quaintly imitated adult sagacity whatever her sharp eyes observed. A historian, having exhausted more sophisticated sources, might read with interest and amusement the comments of this gentle, gifted child on the passing scene.

Around 1825, for example, there was a sudden craze for balloon ascensions. The previous year, Lafayette had returned to America, no more the dashing young general, but a gray and ragged hero who paraded up Broadway under a shower of flowers. He was given the somewhat bizarre honor of cutting the rope which allowed New York's first passenger balloon to ascend gracefully into the skies over the Battery.

In that year an "interesting female" made her ascent from Castle Garden at the Battery and floated over the city, eventually landing somewhat ingloriously in a Long Island pond. Euphemia must have witnessed the beginning of this odd saga for at that time she wrote:

> *Did you see the balloon that went up on Thursday afternoon at four o'clock [she asks her uncle]? Poor Mrs. Joseph could not see it at all. Everybody saw it but her. She is in pain with her eyes. I think it is a great misfortune to have weak eyes but we must take it as God sends it.*

Euphemia took notice of anything concerning her first love, music. Miss Meetz married and went to live abroad as Mrs. Charles Moulton. Euphemia loved her very much and kept up an affectionate correspondence with her in France. At home she now had another teacher, Mr. Gentil. She speaks of her progress, asking Pierre for new pieces of music she wants to learn — "The White Lady," "The Caliph of Bagdad," "Telemaque" and an overture twenty-seven pages long.

She heard that the celebrated Garcia Italian opera troupe was being brought to New York in 1825 by Dominick Lynch Jr. and Lorenzo da Ponte.

*I have heard that the Italian Opera singers have
arrived and you said that when they came you would go
to the theater. I hope I shall be able to go and see them. I
should like to see them very much indeed. I have heard
that they cannot speak any other language than Italian.*

No doubt she knew nothing of the mysterious Da Ponte, friend and one-time collaborator of Mozart. He was a priest in bad standing who had been discovered, hungry and destitute, in a Broadway bookstore by Clement Clarke Moore, author of "The Night before Christmas." Moore, taking pity on the brilliant and unfortunate man, took him to his home and looked after him, eventually gathering together a group of persons interested in studying Italian. Thus Da Ponte was able to make a humble living in America, a sad contrast to his earlier days when he had been a favorite at the court in Vienna. He had been author of the librettos for *Don Giovanni* and *The Marriage of Figaro.*

The Garcia singers were famous throughout Europe and Signor Garcia, their leader, was finally convinced by Da Ponte to make the trip to New York to play before an American audience. Garcia's daughter, Maria Felicita, was the star. Later she was married in St. Peter's Church, New York, and became as famous as Madame Malibran.

Their coming, the first introduction of Italian opera in the United States, proved very successful. Evidently Pierre took Euphemia to hear them perform.

On November 25, 1825, she wrote:

*When we were at the Opera a few nights ago I think
that young lady sung "home sweet home" so sweetly that
I should be very much pleased if you would be so kind*

as to get it for me and I will try to imitate her as much
as I possibly can not only in that song but in all.

Sometimes Pierre must have promised her rewards for doing well at her lessons. Occasionally she scolded him for forgetting to carry out his promises promptly. She wanted him to take her to Brooklyn—quite an expedition before the bridge was built. She wanted to give a party for some children, to be taken visiting—all the simple treats so keenly anticipated by children.

Often she pleaded with childish urgency some little need: a "little girl" (a doll), a piece of muslin to cover her book, a pencil for writing letters, "to have my white frocks altered," or to have her piano repaired. It had been broken by some naughty boy. She heard about the "looking glass curtain" at the Park Theater and begged Pierre to take her there to see *Richard the Third*.

After the consecration of Bishop John Dubois, successor to Bishop Connolly, in October, 1826, she wrote:

Have you seen the new Bishop? I have not seen him
yet. I believe I will go to see him some day at Church.

Bishop Dubois' administration brought a surge of church-building in New York. Euphemia wrote:

I have been to our new Catholic Church in Ann
Street. It is now in an uproar. They are making an altar
and the vestry is fixed differently from Saint Peter's. It
is behind the altar. Mr. Herber is trying to make the
Church beautiful because he is sexton of it and he says
Saint Peter is not so beautiful. It has not so handsome
an organ but I think our little Church is as good as
theirs.

A loyal parishioner! She was a thoughtful child. Her remarks are often philosophical, reflecting no doubt what she had heard Pierre say. Through all her letters we hear echoes of pious phrases, sentiments a child could scarcely have invented. Some recur so often we seem to hear the voice of Pierre using them, as he must have done in his everyday speech.

> *God knows best.*

> *I pray God will conserve you.*

> *We must take it as God gives us with patience and moderation for He does as He pleases whether we like it or not and still He does all for us that is necessary.*

We must take it as God sends it. Over and over, like a broken record, the theme of patience and resignation, peace with one's self and with others.

Maybe sometimes Pierre set too high a standard for her, and she could not always quite come up to the mark:

> *It is true that the time is past when I might have improved myself to a greater advantage but I can't recall it. . . .*

And then too, as one day when rumors of dire things to come flew around her:

> *I have heard that an angel appeared to a watchman and told him that the city of New York was to be destroyed by an earthquake on the 15th of the month and some people say the angel appeared with music but I do not believe it although it has terrified some people very much . . .*

Once she described simply and reverently the meaning of Holy Communion as the reception of the body and blood, soul and divinity of Our Lord.

On Good Friday Juliette took her to Christ Church. She was deeply moved.

> *Week before last you ought to have been to Christ Church. It was beautiful on Good Friday. It was hung so deeply with black, but on Saturday when we were singing Gloria, the black was off in a moment on Easter Sunday.*
>
> *There was most beautiful music. If it had been to save me, I could not have kept my head still from keeping time. There was something at the side altar to represent Our Saviour in his vault. We could see the representation of the dark cloud and the white dress inside just as it said in the evangelist.*
>
> *I should be delighted to see it again. I hope if we live to see next year we will go to that Church.*

CHAPTER 19

THE BITTER BLOW

In 1817 the Sisters of Charity, Mother Seton's daughters, had opened their orphanage in a little wooden house on Prince Street, opposite St. Patrick's Cathedral. At first they took in five homeless children. Very soon they were being forced to turn many away, because of the limitations of their space.

Father Power, an energetic young Irish priest who had become pastor of St. Peter's Church in 1822, undertook, with the encouragement of Bishop Dubois, to do something about the situation. He began giving special money-raising sermons to build a new and roomier orphanage. But the funds came in a slow trickle.

A tremendous help came in the form of a highly successful benefit performance given by the Garcia opera troupe in St. Patrick's Cathedral. It was June, 1826, and according to the *Truth Teller,* New York's newly established Catholic weekly, "the event . . . brought together a crowded and fashionable audience. In addition to a numerous body of the Catholics of this city, there were many of almost every persuasion, as well as a number of strangers who are now visiting New York. Music rolled through the Gothic vaults of the Cathedral with the utmost sublimity. . . . The Italians as well as the other performers handsomely volunteered their services on the occasion and their efforts will be properly appreciated by the whole Catholic community of this city. . ."

The newspaper account did not mention, however, that St. Patrick's choir, not quite appreciative of the "utmost sublimity" of the Italian singers, resigned in a body on the occasion in protest against some real or imagined slight. However, the benefit was a huge success and Father Power was able to build his new orphanage, the three-story structure he had dreamed of, with room for one hundred and fifty children. Pierre's efforts as ticket seller had helped with the success of the project.

Each year on her name day, September 16, Pierre would take Euphemia to the orphanage for a visit. On the way they always stopped at the bakery and filled a big basket with buns, gingerbread, and "jumbles" as treats for the nuns to distribute among the children.

After one of these trips, Euphemia wrote to her uncle:

> When we were at the orphan asylum how glad they
> seemed to be when they saw the cakes. There was a little
> girl there. I do not believe she was but three years old.
> She was a very nice little thing. I should be very glad to
> have them all come here and take tea some afternoon.

Even Juliette's famous hospitality would hardly have been equal to that occasion!

A friend once asked Pierre, "Does Euphemia pass out the

cakes herself to the children?"

"Oh no," was the answer. "That would not be proper for a little black girl. We give them to the Sisters to distribute."

One day, coming home from the orphanage, Euphemia asked her uncle quite innocently.

"What are orphans?"

"They are poor little children who have no father or mother," Pierre explained.

For a moment Euphemia looked quite sad. Then she smiled.

"But have they no uncle?"

Pierre would tell this story for years to come, always adding:

"I thanked God with all my heart."

Euphemia, an orphan herself, had never known the loss of her real parents.

On January 1, 1829, Euphemia sat down to compose her New Year's greeting to her uncle Pierre. She was fourteen years old, and could express herself quite fluently.

She had tried so often before to tell him just how she felt about him, how good he had been to her, but she could never make it sound right. This time, she would try even harder. All day she had been making it up in her mind, choosing the phrases she would use. Now she knew exactly what she wanted to say.

> *Dear Uncle*
>
> *Will you be pleased to accept my most respectful compliments on the close of the old and the commencement of the new year. Give me leave, dear Uncle, to tell you as well as my poor mind can express itself how truly sensible I am of all your favors. I will try by my conduct to merit the continuance of them.*

*As it has pleased God to give you good health during
the course of the last year, I beseech Him to grant you
the same to the end of the present and many more, my
prayers are morning and night offered up to Heaven for
your preservation. Nor are you ever in the day absent
from my thoughts.*

I remain your dutiful niece,

Euphemia Toussaint.

Stilted and stiff, in the very correct and formal usage of her nineteenth-century lesson books, she tried to tell him of the gratitude that was in her heart. She knew now what an orphan was, and that without Pierre she would have had no father. Nor could any parents have done more for their own daughter than Juliette and Pierre had done for her.

Pierre could not help being affected when he read what his niece had written so neatly and carefully. New Year's Day —a day of fresh beginnings, fresh hopes. It was not just the letter, but something Juliette had said to him only that morning. Something was worrying her. Euphemia seemed always so tired, as if everything were too great an effort. And for the past few days, she had had a little fever, not much, but . . .

"Probably just another cold," Pierre spoke to reassure Juliette. "Just the same, let's have Dr. Berger, and see what he says."

But Juliette was suspicious. She had seen too much of this particular illness not to know its signs. And she was afraid that Euphemia's old disease, tuberculosis, had come back.

Once again Dr. Berger shook his head and spoke very gravely. This time there could be no hope, however faint. A few months at the most, and this beloved child would no longer be with them.

So often in her little weekly notes to Pierre she had used the phrase "if we live to see next year." A childish repetition? Or an intimation of death. Nevertheless he and Juliette did not tell Euphemia how serious her condition was.

Later on Euphemia stayed in bed, but she did not appear very ill. It was a blessing that she felt no pain, hardly any discomfort. The illness advanced with terrible speed, yet so stealthily she only seemed to be wasting away. Pierre and Juliette had tried to teach Euphemia all she would need to know for a useful and a Christian life. But now they saw, heartbroken, that it had not been for this world that they had prepared her after all.

Pierre, who had watched by many deathbeds, knew that once again, in His mysterious plan, God would soon take a loved one from him. He tried to prepare himself. He loved her so much, too much perhaps, for a man who loved so deeply might want to keep for himself the one he loved. But God would see to that as He had done before.

He was stricken. He could not face it. Neither could he rebel.

"I thank God for all His goodness," was his sorrowful comment. "He is good. We know it here. But my Euphemia," he pointed upward, "will be the first to know it there."

Euphemia's last days passed happily. Pierre would sit by the hour as she lay propped up on her pillows, reading to her and showing her all the little gifts and remembrances with which his friends showered her. She would lie in his arms and talk about all she would do for her uncle when she was well again. He knew differently. Perhaps she did too.

Flowers, candies, toys—Pierre would amuse her by counting and recounting all her treasures strewn about the bed.

"I make Uncle eat all these up," she said playfully, "but I

keep the flowers, just to look at."

Like a flower, symbol of beauty and contemplation, had been the short life of this child. Father Power came often to the house until the end. Pierre, who had consoled so many, had now to be consoled.

Euphemia died on May 11, 1829. Once she had told Pierre in a letter that "we are made of dust and we shall return to it." Her body was laid in St. Patrick's cemetery.

Pierre could find no rest night or day. He had watched over the child with such intensity. Now her going seemed to threaten his very life. He did not want to see anyone, or go out anywhere. His friends stood by and watched helplessly as he struggled, weary and gaunt with grief, to control himself and go about his work as usual.

It was a bitter conflict. Never before had he wished to withhold anything from God. Her name was almost unbearable to him. Hearing it, he would cover his face with his hands and say, "My poor Euphemia is gone."

His friends saw with alarm that the strong Toussaint, the courageous, seemed to have loosed his own strong hold on life. Each day he tried mechanically to go out to his work, returning at night to a home desolate in all but memories. Juliette was terribly worried about him. Those who were close to him plied him for a long time with unremitting consolations. He read and reread their letters. Like a blind man trying to learn to read by fingering braille, his stunned mind gradually pieced together the truth they had been repeating: that Euphemia could hardly be better off with him than where she now was. And God, who saw Pierre broken in all but faith, poured sweet comfort into the words of those who sought to console him.

Some of the letters they wrote him at this time were

beautiful indeed. Here is Mrs. Cruger's:

> *I need not say, my dear Toussaint, how much I*
> *sympathize with you; my heart and soul follow you in*
> *your last cares for this cherished child, to whom you*
> *have ever been the best, the most tender of fathers. . . .*
> *But I could not weep for her, I wept for you . . .*
>
> *The life of Euphemia has been almost a miracle;*
> *she owes her existence to your constant care and*
> *watchfulness. Her short life has been full of happiness;*
> *she has never known the loss of a mother; far happier*
> *than hundreds of others raised in the wealthiest and*
> *most elevated classes, the most gentle virtues and*
> *affections have surrounded her from her cradle, and she*
> *has been taken from a paradise on earth to enter into an*
> *eternity of happiness . . .*

And Mary Anne Schuyler, from her country home in
Rhinebeck, thought of him constantly. She knew him so
well, and all that he endured.

> *. . . my dear Toussaint, as I write you the remembrance*
> *of your beloved Euphemia presses upon my heart at the*
> *meek submission with which you yielded her to her God*
> *who has taken her to Himself. Surely she has escaped*
> *from the strong wind and the tempest and we will not*
> *repine. But she has been removed from her earthly*
> *parents to her Father in Heaven, safe from sin and*
> *temptation. . . .*

That year the springtime passed by unnoticed. Time the
healer was slow in answering this summons. July brought a
letter, so far as we know the last one, from Gabriel Nicolas.

I have received your letter, my dear Toussaint, and share very deeply the sorrow which the loss of your niece must bring upon you. No one knows better than I, how much you were attached to her. However, as you say very truly, we must resign ourselves to the will of God. I am sorry to hear that Juliette has been ill, and hope that your next letter will speak of her re-established health.

I have not written you for a long time, my dear Toussaint, not that I do not think of you, or that I love you less, but I was troubled because I was not able to send you anything. However I know your heart, and feel quite sure you will not attribute this delay to lack of inclination. You have no idea how unhappy I am when I cannot meet little debts.

But, my dear Toussaint, I fail every day. I am at least ten years older than when I last saw you. Both courage and strength begin to fail, and to add to all this, I do not hear a word from France about our claims. You can understand my sad situation. But a few years longer will put an end to my misery. However I do not despair to see you again before. . . .

Even for another's sorrow, Gabriel could not long forget his own. And Pierre had played for so long the role of the consoler, the parts of the various players could not be immediately recast.

Juliette's grief over Euphemia's death was amplified by her own subsequent illness, no doubt brought on by the strain and fatigue of caring for the child during those last months. And she was very much alarmed over Toussaint's extreme prostration. Never before had she seen him lose command of his feelings. People reminded him gently of the anxiety he was causing her, a worry which was to last for another year.

Like a man in danger of plunging into an abyss, he clung desperately to a fingerhold. That fingerhold was his daily visit to St. Peter's Church. He tried to pray harder than ever; when he could not pray, he waited patiently before the tabernacle. Outside, he looked for others on whom to lavish his love.

He redoubled his work for the orphans. More than ten years had passed since the opening of the orphanage, and the Sisters now were caring for over a hundred children.

Twice childless, he still was to find in children the main outlet for his grief. The orphans needed him and he needed them. His work for them became a dedication. Now the "little black girl" with the big basket of sweets was gone, but Toussaint came to them, and would always come, with even greater gifts.

CHAPTER 20

STEWARD OVER MANY

Among the remarkable gifts Euphemia had received from her foster parents had been her education. Just one generation removed from slavery, she had been carefully tutored in French and English conversation as well as composition, and in mathematics. Her letters showed familiarity with the Church's teachings and her rites. She had had music lessons from qualified teachers. Pierre had passed on to her his courtesy and consideration for the feelings of others. Juliette had given her practiced instruction in the domestic arts.

Certainly Euphemia had been especially privileged in this respect. There were few educational opportunities for black children in the days when she lived. Yet Pierre, looking back over his own life and the profits of his own early reading, was a firm advocate of education. He and Juliette had been happy to turn their own home into a school of sorts for the training, through the years, of a succession of otherwise neglected black boys. Now another opportunity came, this time to Juliette, to help found a school for the black children of Baltimore, where she had many relatives.

In that city a small group of working girls, four in all, refugees from Saint Domingue, had formed in 1829 a religious society to aid the abandoned children of their race. The Oblate Sisters of Providence, first religious community for black women in the world, began under the inspiration of a Sulpician Father of noble French lineage: Jacques Marie Joubert de la Muraille.

Since the opening of their seminary, during the French Revolution, the Sulpicians had been gathering together for Sunday Mass the black Catholics of Baltimore, and had administered the sacraments to them regularly. The catechism classes begun around 1796 by Father William Dubourg had been carried on later by Father Jean Marie Tessier, and now had become the responsibility of Father Joubert.

He soon saw to his dismay that his efforts were being rendered almost futile by the fact that the children who gathered before him each week in the *chapelle basse* of St. Mary's Seminary were illiterate. It was a story of sheer neglect. The grandparents of these youngsters might have brought considerable culture with them from Saint Domingue, but here in America they had been forced to labor long and hard for a living. There had been no time, money or strength left for the teaching of the younger generation. Baltimore had no school yet for them.

Thus was born the idea of a religious community devoted exclusively to the teaching of black children. Under Father Joubert's encouragement and sound direction the four original Oblates had courageously established their foundation and were living in community. They already had a few pupils.

It was a daring project. In October, 1829, that first difficult year, five bishops and one archbishop met at Baltimore for the First Provincial Council in the United States. And the rented house of the Oblates on George Street, where the nuns had taken their first vows, was a high point on the itinerary of the visiting prelates. They wanted to see the country's first Catholic school for black children. When they had inspected and approved of everything, even the drawings of the children, they were preparing to leave. Bishop Flaget of Bardstown, the eldest among them, was asked to give the nuns his blessing. Raising his hands to do so, the venerable priest suddenly paused and spoke to them mysteriously:

"You are yet only four; in two years you shall be twelve. In the name of the Father and of the Son and of the Holy Ghost, Amen."

His words proved to be prophetic.

Juliette's cousin, Fanny Montpensier, was one of the Oblates' enthusiastic supporters from the first. She worked in the Baltimore household of a Madame DeLarue, and through Fanny's frequent letters to Juliette we glimpse the early struggles and triumphs of the pioneer community. Fanny Montpensier was apparently one of those staunch and tireless souls who quickly become pillars of whatever cause they choose to support. She was not at all hesitant about begging help for the nuns, and Juliette was often called upon to lend a hand.

"Mr. [Father] Deluol," Fanny wrote to Juliette in June, 1832, "yesterday, gave me the eighteen *gourdes* you sent him. I gave them to Mr. Joubert who thanks you as do the Sisters. They won't fail to think of you in their prayers."

The spirit of self-sacrifice shown by the Oblates was an understandable source of encouragement to other black

Catholics. In one of her letters of 1832, Fanny tells of the heroic death of Sister Antoine, her close friend, during the cholera epidemic. Sister Antoine had volunteered to nurse Archbishop Eccleston through an attack of this plague, later returning to the Bishop's house to care for his housekeeper. This time Sister Antoine was also stricken and died within fourteen hours.

From time to time Juliette visited Baltimore, renewing acquaintances, visiting her many relatives, the Noel and Avieux families, and, of course, the Oblates. There she could enjoy the pleasure of hearing a good French sermon, an experience now becoming rare in New York as the Irish influence grew stronger and stronger.

Like all good housewives, who must fret a little when they are away from home, Juliette probably worried a bit about the Reade Street household while she was not there. During one of her Baltimore sojourns, Pierre wrote this note to reassure her.

> My dearly beloved:
>
> I have just received your letter and am replying immediately. I am very sorry you had this villainous attack. I hope you are better. I beg the good Lord you do not fall ill and become a burden to your friends. Mr. [Father] Hérard came here yesterday and slept here and has just left. The house is in good order and I am well, thank God. . . .

Father Hérard, Pierre's overnight guest during Juliette's absence, was a priest stationed at Bottle Hill, New Jersey. Pierre was always doing some little favor for him. The Toussaint house was a halfway station for Father Hérard's mail, books and packages. From Baltimore, then the church goods center of the country, shipments of medals, crucifixes, music books, and catechisms often arrived at Reade Street to be forwarded to Father Hérard. Sometimes they were accompanied by notes from priests at St. Mary's Seminary, with directions for their delivery.

Fanny Montpensier, in her zeal to provide the Oblate Sisters and the orphans in their charge with every necessity, often made good use of Juliette's well-known good taste and shopping sagacity. She sent to New York requests for clothing materials, shoes, even food. Nor would she be content to leave the choices and the bargaining to Juliette. Every desired item was described to the last detail, so that Juliette would have to spend considerable time whenever she went on a shopping trip for Fanny.

In one hastily written letter Fanny asks for "three rock fish about three quarters of a yard long, two fresh codfish about the same size, but must be clean, four black fish, very nice, and two dozen very fresh lobsters."

Then she added explicit shipping instructions.

> *Buy a box or crate, whichever you find most convenient, which will hold them all. Put a little ice with them to preserve them, arrange them as best you can and address it Reverend Mr. Deluol, St. Mary's College, Baltimore. Send it by stage.*
>
> *You will receive this letter tomorrow. I hope you will be able to do it on Tuesday. They must arrive in Baltimore Wednesday night or Thursday morning at the latest. If you cannot send them on that day, it is of no use to buy them . . . add up your expenses, cost of letters, purchases, and all, and Mr. Deluol will give orders to the Sisters of Charity in New York to repay you.*
>
> *You will oblige him very much if you can do it, and me also.*

Then, realizing she is being quite demanding, Fanny adds, apologetically:

I think my dear friend Toussaint will not be displeased with the trouble I give you. Adieu. I embrace you all.

The Sisters of Charity at the Prince Street orphanage in New York had come from their motherhouse at Emmitsburg, which was under the direction of the Sulpician Fathers. It was therefore an easy matter for Father Deluol to send Juliette the money through the Sisters in New York. Pierre probably found it waiting one day when he went on his regular trip to the orphanage to turn in his collection.

In another request Fanny commissioned Juliette to buy four lengths of French calico "of a small rose pattern" and other colors for making children's clothes, "and fourteen yards of a larger design for grown-up persons."

With the utmost consideration for the nuns' tiny budget, Fanny added firmly: "For the calico, you must not pay more than three shillings or three shillings six cents."

So in New York with its ever-increasing shops and variety of goods, Juliette would often exercise her economy in buying for the orphan children of her own race in Baltimore. In her letters to Fanny she very often sent her own offerings for the nuns. They were trying to raise funds for a chapel. It would be the first building erected in the United States for religious services for black Catholics.

Again, history in the making. But Pierre and Juliette seemed destined to be close to many beginnings. Progress was quickening all around them. Already the inventive genius that was to symbolize America had been at work, and no place had it been more in evidence than in the Stevens family.

John C. Stevens was a partner of Philip Jeremiah Schuyler in a quarry business on the shores of the Hudson. Pierre was for years coiffeur as well as close friend of both Mrs. Schuyler and Mrs. Stevens, and therefore a daily visitor to their homes. He had known the interest with which both men had watched the exciting experiments made by the elder Colonel John Stevens in steam navigation. After the completion of his service as treasurer of the Continental Army, Colonel Stevens had developed an ingenious, if inadequate, system of wooden water mains for New York City. When the steamboat had become a reality, the Stevens family enterprisingly set up a ferry service from New York to Hoboken. And to attract holidaying city dwellers in search of fresher country air, they had turned part of their country estate at Hoboken, now the site of Stevens Institute, into an amusement park: the Elysian Fields. Here the great American sport of baseball first had been organized, and cricket games introduced to curious spectators from Manhattan.

Along with the development of steam transportation had come another innovation: the opening of the Erie Canal in 1825, linking the Hudson River with the Great Lakes. It was then that the great distances of the North American continent had begun to grow smaller, and on her horizon the *ignis fatuus*—a dream of boundless speed—had begun to glow tantalizingly before the eyes of daring men.

In the early years of the century, Alexander Hamilton could easily complete the writing of an issue of *The Federalist* during the leisurely one-week trip from New York to the Albany home of his father-in-law. General Schuyler. Now, in 1851, another Schuyler was enthusiastically helping establish speed records in steamboat travel through the inland waters that had once seemed so remote to New Yorkers. He was George Lee, eldest son of Philip Jeremiah and Mary Anne Schuyler. Here is a letter written by the venturesome young man on one of his experimental cruises.

S.S. Magnolia, Ohio River,
May 6, 1831

I received your letter of February 27, my dear brother Toussaint, with the greatest possible pleasure. We are at present on the Ohio River which the French have rightly named the Beautiful River.

We set out from Cincinnati the day before yesterday and we shall arrive at Pittsburgh Sunday morning. That finished, we shall have made 2000 miles almost, by steamboat, without an accident. In five or six days we shall be at Niagara, and from there it will be a very short business going to New York. We can make it in four days but as we are traveling very pleasantly we shall take ten or twelve days.

We have seen a lot and when I see you, I will have many things to tell you. I haven't written them in my letter for I find I have forgotten almost all my French. For that reason I beg you to show this to no one, except those who do not know French!

We have received no news of Madame Cruger for two or three weeks. I hope she and all the family are in good health. Doubtless the winter has been very long and sad for them. I am very anxious to see them, above all, Mademoiselle Henrietta.

I have made the acquaintance of many pretty young ladies, and I have lost my heart in New Orleans, on board the steamboat on the Mississippi, to a young lady,

and a widow at Louisville, and to another at Cincinnati.
If I ever return to this country I shall not dare appear
before any of these five ladies. . . .

We are at present all in good health but my father
had an attack of gout at Cincinnati and all except
myself have had attacks of stomach trouble. Now all this
is past.

Give my regards to Madame Juliette and to everyone
I know in New York. They are calling us to dinner now
and as I always have a big appetite on the water, I must
finish this letter. Mama sends you a thousand regards.

I am, always, your friend
George L. Schuyler.

Yachting too was an enthusiasm of the first families.
When John C. Stevens' *Wave* was put into the water in 1832,
American yachting had really begun. A few such vessels had
appeared before, but no great racing yacht had been launched.
It would be another twelve years before the first yacht club was
founded at the Elysian Fields in Hoboken. Eventually George
Lee Schuyler and John C. Stevens would bring the America
Cup to this country, defeating England's best yacht.

Pierre must have followed all these developments closely,
for they were often discussed in the Stevens and Schuyler
households. Members of both families found it quite natural
to keep in touch with him by letter whenever they went
traveling.

How did Pierre keep up such a wide correspondence? Did
he work all day and write all night? Certainly many times
he must have been wearied answering the endless letters
that came to him. Around the 1830's his writing changed
from the perfect fluid writing of the younger Toussaint to a

cramped and heavy hand.

Still the letters kept coming. Priests, former customers, old friends; they were certain to keep in touch with Pierre. And another kind of letter never stopped either: the short begging notes from persons who are only names, the names of countless human needs, of manifold distress. Sophia Kearns begged for a loan of ten dollars. Her husband was very ill. Someone named Zephire sought a loan for a friend, incurably afflicted, who hoped to start up a small *boutique* and make his own living. Some of these demands were even a bit imperious. One man informed Pierre that he needed one hundred dollars, and right away too, so would Pierre kindly remit by return post. It was to pay his family's passage back to America from France.

Some of the letters brought Pierre sadness, like the one that came from Paris in the summer of 1834. It was written by Madame de Berty, Aurore Bérard's sister.

> *You are already in sorrow, my dear Toussaint, and the sad news I must announce to you will only augment it. Two months have passed since your beloved godmother was taken from us by sudden death.*
>
> *My heart is so deeply oppressed by the affliction, that I can scarcely write. A few days before her death she spoke of you. She wished to write to you, being very anxious at not having heard from you for a long time.*
>
> *What pleasure she would have experienced in receiving your last letter, which arrived about fifteen days since!*
>
> *. . . I hope your dear godmother now enjoys perfect happiness. Since the death of our parents she has suffered much . . . Her patience and her resignation to the will of God, and her entire confidence in the Mother of God, will be her propitiation.*

So that chapter closed. The valley of L'Artibonite seemed very distant in time and space. It was a strange valley now, perhaps unrecognizable. No voices spoke to him from there any more. Pierre's last link with his earliest years was broken.

Since 1815 he had heard no definite word of his mother. But he always kept up his support of the women from the old plantation, former slaves who had found themselves less resourceful than himself.

Faithful over a few things in the beginning, Pierre was now steward over many. Providence had placed at his command the means to assist others, and he never faltered in his administration of these goods-in-trust. His charities reached out in many directions, some becoming known after the way of man's justice, some remaining secret, after the way of God's.

A friend asked him half-seriously:

"Toussaint, you are the richest man I know. You have more than you want. Why not stop working?"

Pierre's answer was simple.

"Then, Madame, I should not have enough for others!"

CHAPTER 21

1835-1842

L e jour de l'an! The year 1835 was only a few hours old, and the snow, falling lightly, had hardly finished covering the erratic tracks of the evening's last revelers. Pierre stepped from his doorway into a white and trailless world. His footprints would be the first that morning to thread upon the background of a snow-covered city the tortuous back-and-forth weave of human pilgrimage.

Pierre was sixty-eight now, almost half a century away from the tropics. But snow still had a strangeness about it, especially in the stillness of this hour. He had promised to be at the Schuylers' earlier today, to dress Mrs. Schuyler's hair in time to receive her New Year's callers.

He made his way along Canal Street and turned in at the Philip Schuyler house. The young son of the family, George Lee, greeted him at the door.

"Bonne année, Pierre!"

"A happy New Year to you, Monsieur George," Pierre

replied. "I promised your mother I would come first thing this morning—"

"Good! Then she will be expecting you. She needs a visit from you right now. Father had a pretty bad night."

"Oh, I'm sorry to hear it. Your poor mother must be quite worn out."

"She is. In fact she was so upset she sent one of the servants to call me during the night. But Father is resting more easily just now. I think I'll be going back to Laight Street. Eliza will be waiting."

George Lee was twenty-three. He had recently been married to Eliza Hamilton, daughter of Alexander Hamilton's third son James Alexander. Pierre had known both of the young people since their childhood, and had been their lifetime confidant.

"Frances, take Toussaint's coat," George Lee spoke to a servant who stepped forward, exchanging greetings with Pierre at the same time.

The servant went upstairs to tell Mrs. Schuyler of the hairdresser's arrival. Pierre stepped to the back of the house to give New Year's greetings to the other servants. He had been coming to the Schuylers' for over fifteen years now, whenever they were in residence in the city, and he never missed having a chat with each member of the household on his daily visits. Even when the Schuylers were staying at their country estate, Rhinebeck, on the Hudson, the same close association existed, for Mrs. Schuyler seldom let many days pass without sending a note or letter to Pierre.

Today she was feeling very weary, but she brightened up and smiled as he entered the room.

"Good morning, Madame." Pierre spoke gently. "And may the New Year bring you many blessings—especially better health to Monsieur Schuyler."

Mrs. Schuyler held up the hand mirror and studied her own face quizzically for a moment.

"Hardly a face to greet New Year's visitors with, is it, Pierre? This will call for every bit of skill you possess, but — 'what custom bids, in all things we must do,' " she quoted philosophically.

"Just wait, Madame. Toussaint can fix that very easily." She did look tired, but he would try a little different arrangement of her hair today, perhaps a bit more youthful, to offset the shadows on her rather plump face.

"Monsieur George tells me Monsieur Schuyler did not rest well last night. How is he?"

"Oh, sleeping just now, poor man. But the pain grows worse. He always seems to feel better when we are at Rhinebeck, but then, the weather is so bad, I wouldn't think of trying to go up."

"But spring isn't far away, Madame. Then you can go."

"Yes, that's all I am looking forward to, these days. Pierre, I wish you would promise to come up to Rhinebeck and spend some time this summer, you and Juliette." It was an invitation she repeated often, but Pierre's many obligations never seemed to leave him any leisure for a trip.

Forced into retirement by his poor health, Philip Schuyler and his wife took frequent trips nowadays to various resorts in search of relief from his ailments. On these journeys Pierre was always on Mrs. Schuyler's mind, and she wrote him countless little notes, sometimes addressing them quaintly to "Mr. Toussaint, Ladies' Hairdresser, Reade Street near Chapel, left hand from Broadway, New York."

Once when they were vacationing in Baden-Baden, this good Protestant lady sent Pierre a message through her son

Robert:

> *They have an English service every Sunday here,*
> *to which I am now going all by myself. The service is*
> *performed in a Catholic chapel with all the insignia.*
> *I thought of my dear Toussaint and I send my love to*
> *him—tell him I think of him very often—I never go into*
> *one of the churches of his own faith without remember-*
> *ing my own St. Pierre and nobody has a better saint.*
>
> *I am pleased to hear that he is better, and his good*
> *Juliette. Read this to my Toussaint and may God bless*
> *him forever.*

One little difficulty bothered her in letter writing. Pierre much preferred reading French, but she did not feel her French was very fluent, and often apologized for it. From Ballston Spa, where she had taken Philip, she wrote briefly:

> *We are very pleasantly situated and if I could write*
> *in your language I would give you a long letter. As it is*
> *I am afraid of troubling you. Remember me very kindly*
> *to Madame your femme. . . .*

Although she was often a participant in gay social events, the company she found there never seemed quite satisfying. There was always Pierre to turn to, and then she could speak most freely. This was written in Charleston:

> *A word to you in the greatest haste—in a few min-*
> *utes we must be on board Mr. Stevens' boat. We sail*
> *swiftly. Your letter was charming. Mr. Robert is finely.*
> *Heaven listens to the prayers of the good and pious*
> *Toussaint. Say the kindest words to Juliette for us both.*
> *Say to Mr. Stevens I have attended the races and wished*
> *he was at my side to tell me how to bet. . . . Haste, haste,*
> *adieu my good friend,*

Yours forever,
M.A.S.

It was her customary signature.

She admitted she was "a nervous lady." Sometimes anxiety shows very clearly in her messages.

> *My dear St. Pierre:*
>   *I expected you all of yesterday morning and as you did not come I have worried myself into the belief that you are again lame. I am sure if you or Juliette had been very ill you would have sent me word. I dreamt of you last night... .*

Philip Schuyler had lived all his life in close association with many of America's greatest personalities. Now, looking back over his active years, he made a startling statement which was repeated to his children and grandchildren until it became a legend.

"I have known Christians who were not gentlemen, gentlemen who were not Christians—but one man I know who is both—and that man is black!"

On the bitterly cold night of December 16, 1835, a terrible fire swept through a great part of New York's business district. Twenty million dollars' worth of buildings and merchandise disappeared before the eyes of their horror-stricken owners as if by some gruesome magic. The rivers were frozen over, and even if there had been water, the hand engines could have done little against the raging flames.

Panicky fire fighters, summoned from all the surrounding area, even from New Jersey, blew up building after building in a crazed attempt to control the blaze. Seven hundred buildings—nearly all of New York's business district—were destroyed that night, including the Merchants' Exchange, hub of New York commerce, which had been completed only eight years before. Its commanding dome, on Wall Street east of The Broadway, crashed in ruins before the shivering watchers. Sparks flew on the frigid wind across the East River to Brooklyn, where fearful householders spent all that night wetting their vulnerable shingled roofs against the infernal shower.

Next morning hundreds woke to find themselves bankrupt through the failure of businesses and insurance firms. Scores of merchants met financial ruin. It was the worst catastrophe, economically, the city had known.

Pierre was among those whose savings were largely lost. Some of his friends immediately wanted to start a subscription for him but Pierre would not hear of such a thing.

"I do not need it," he insisted. "Others are far more in want of it than I am."

Quite detached from his own loss, despite the fact that he was getting along in years and would not be able to replace a lifetime's savings, he went early that morning to console a friend he knew must have suffered a severe financial setback in the last few hours. The lady later told of that memorable visit:

"The great fire of 1835 changed our fortunes. The first person who came to us early the next morning was Toussaint, to proffer his services and sympathy."

Physically, Pierre's world was a small one. But his charities still flew, like winged flocks, to far places. His eyes looked out upon the porches and roofs and back yards of one city. His heart looked out upon a world where, no matter how distant, someone called out for help.

Some of these whose voices he heard were members of

the clergy like Michael McDonnell, a seminarian at St. Hyacinth College, Montreal. He writes to thank Pierre for past kindnesses:

> ... the increasing feebleness of my health has obliged me to make over to another ecclesiastic a large part of my work ... You will understand that the work being diminished by half, it necessarily follows ... that the salary should also be diminished in proportion ... so that consequently, while others have 50 dollars, I find myself reduced to the small sum of 25 dollars, with which to clothe myself and furnish everything required for my studies, as well as to meet all my other necessities.
>
> My dear friend, I find myself at the approach of a severe winter without the clothing necessary to protect me against its rigorous blasts. ...

A homesick French priest wrote a pathetic note asking help in getting back to Paris: "If I remain longer at New York, I shall be miserable."

Another priest, whose writing is all but illegible, wrote from the island of Saint Lucia, *"Antilles anglaises"* to ask Pierre to thank Father Power of St. Peter's for his kind recommendations to the local bishops, who had received him very hospitably.

Many families kept in touch with Pierre from France. Among these were the aristocratic Lagnels. One of the Lagnel sons, Alfred, was a regular correspondent. In March, 1836, he wrote from his home at 22 Rue Louis le Grand:

> I delivered immediately your messages to M. and Mme. de Neuville who are now here with all their brother's family. It gave them great pleasure to get news from you, and they begged me to tell you so. ... Mme. Juel of New

York will also pass the summer in the United States. She goes with her grandson and her son-in-law, M. LeRay de Chaumont. . . .

We will have here for some weeks longer, the venerable M. de Cheverus, formerly Bishop of Boston, now Archbishop of Bordeaux, and who has just been raised to the rank of Cardinal. This holy man, worthy prince of the Church, is always the same, a living image of the Apostles in simplicity and self-abnegation. I have met him in the streets of Bordeaux, having under his arm a package of clothing which he was carrying to the poor. It is a most providential thing for them, for all his acts bear the same stamp of goodness, and devotion to the unfortunate.

Adieu (or farewell) my dear good Toussaint. Write to me when you have a moment to spare, and do not forget to let me know whatever you can learn about Jules.

Jules was a brother of Alfred, who had come over to attend West Point. The third brother, Numa, also came to the Academy, bringing, as an introduction, a letter from the Marquis de Lafayette. Alfred was serving as secretary to Hyde de Neuville, former French Ambassador to the United States.

Pierre also always maintained a keen interest in Church affairs on his native island. After the revolt, there had been great confusion in ecclesiastical jurisdictions. The Holy See had refused to recognize priests approved by the Haitian government. After prolonged negotiations, often broken off for long periods, an agreement was reached whereby priests acceptable to Church authorities were allowed to carry on their work.

One of these, a friend of Pierre's, was Father George Paddington, who went to Haiti as a seminarian and was ordained there.

In 1836, he wrote from Haiti:

> *It would have given me great pleasure to see you again in New York but the President and the Bishop (Bishop John England of Charleston) did not wish me to leave the country to finish my studies in Rome and in France. I was ordained Subdeacon on the 13th instant and immediately after my Ordination, the President sent to tell the Bishop that he had appointed me as professor in the new college of La Coupe, eight miles from the city.*
>
> *The Bishop returned to Charleston last week and I remain here probably for the rest of my life. ... The country and the people are I think the finest and kindest ever met with and I have no doubt but that if faithfully served by good ministers of religion and other instructors, they would become the best people I know of.*

Later that year he was ordained priest by Bishop England in the church at Port-au-Prince.

> *I said my first Mass on Trinity Sunday and rest assured that I did not, nor can I ever forget my friends whenever I celebrate the divine mysteries, among whom I shall always consider you and Madame Toussaint, as particularly dear to me. I celebrated one Mass for you and Madame Toussaint about ten days ago. . . .*
>
> *I was sorry to hear that the roof of your favorite Church had fallen in. Thank God that neither you nor any of the Congregation were in at the time, and I hope that the people will come forward with piety and liberality to build a new and more elegant temple to God in the same place, and that quickly.*

The last Mass in old St. Peter's was celebrated on August

28, 1836, and the building, declared structurally unsafe, was torn down to make room for the new church. New York's first Catholic burial ground, which had surrounded the original church, had to be used for the new foundations, and many of the remains were transferred uptown to the cathedral ground.

On February 25, 1838, the new church, built in Grecian style, was solemnly blessed by Coadjutor Bishop Hughes. Now the parish had a crushing debt that would weigh heavily upon its pastor, Father Power, and the trustees. Pierre's papers include calls to meetings to undertake ways and means of meeting the heavy financial burden.

Pierre had always been active in parish activities. He was a member of the Society of St. Peter and the Society of the Blessed Sacrament. His papers show he attended various organ concerts and other benefits. There are two receipts for pew rent, for the years 1822 and 1842, signed by Sexton James Thiel.

In 1841, he was present in the church when the Count de Forbin-Janson, bishop of Nancy, came as a guest preacher to conduct a mission there. There was now taking place a remarkable revival of Catholicism in France. Much of the leadership in this movement of renewed faith had been taken by Jean Baptist Rantzau, founder of the Society of the Missions of France. In this admirable work of zeal, Charles-Auguste Count de Forbin-Janson was an invaluable aide.

On February 21, concluding his mission at St. Peter's with a stirring sermon, the bishop said:

> *"In this great city of New York where Catholics of*
> *Irish and German birth have hesitated at no sacrifice*
> *to secure churches and priests of their own nationality,*

how is it possible that the French, so famous for the faith
of their fathers, should have remained so indifferent?
They are lacking in interest both for their own salvation
and for that of their countrymen. In truth, how can
they hope to maintain their traditions on a foreign soil
without the strong ties of religion? Such a church is
desired most strongly by Bishop Hughes, who expects
great things for his diocese from it."

Immediately afterward Toussaint presented his donation for the building of the French church in New York. His one hundred dollars was the first contribution received for St. Vincent de Paul Church, first located on Canal Street, and later on West 23rd Street.

Pierre's memories of his native land were sharp and clear, but he could not realize perhaps how much it had changed in his absence, the victim of carnage by man and the elements. In May, 1842, came the worst disaster of all, the great earthquake that fell just short of shattering Haiti and thrusting her into the sea. Pierre received a vivid account of this from one of his correspondents there.

My dear friend, do you know (unhappy country!)
that there exists no longer Cap Haitien; nor Santiago,
nor Port-au-Paix! These three cities were destroyed on
the 7th of May last, by an earthquake. While I speak of
it, my hair stands on end.

Never has living soul seen such a terrible earthquake!
Santiago, such a pretty city, so well built, all with walls
like the Cape, all houses of two or three stories high, all
has been thrown down in half a second. At the Cape not
a house stands upright.

The trembling lasted for five minutes, rapidly, with great force. At Gonnaive the earth opened, and a clear stream of water rushed out. At the same time a fire broke out and consumed twenty houses.

At Port-au-Paix the sea rose violently nearly five feet, and carried off the rest of the houses which had not fallen. At the Cape six thousand persons have been killed under the ruins, and two thousand wounded. At St. Domingo, all the houses have not fallen. They are, however, nearly all shattered and uninhabitable. The shock was much more violent towards the north than at the south; but this gives you some idea of what has taken place in this poor country.

It happened at half past five in the evening. This country is now almost miserable.

Some of Juliette's Baltimore acquaintances were injured and one of them was lost in this tragedy, having returned to the island shortly before. Relatives of the Oblate Sisters also perished there, and in August, 1842, Fanny Montpensier tells of a Mass for the earthquake victims in the Oblate chapel. Pierre's letters at this time show that his wide acquaintance made him a sort of clearinghouse for information on persons missing in the disaster.

CHAPTER 22

TOUSSAINT DRAWS HIS WILL

Of Courtesy, it is much less
Than Courage of Heart or Holiness,
Yet in my walks it seems to me
That the grace of God is in Courtesy.

HILAIRE BELLOC

A twentieth-century quatrain, but a seventeenth-century theme! People had sometimes remonstrated with the bishop of Geneva, Francis de Sales, for his remarkable gentleness. After him, waves of violence had washed over the world, over France. And when the fury stilled, oddly enough, it was the quiet voice of De Sales that stirred the beaten air. Everyone knew and quoted his mild wisdom: You can catch more flies with a spoonful of honey than with a barrel of vinegar.

Pierre must have heard that homely phrase many times,

for in the French homes he visited it was a basic rule of etiquette. Each family had its *Introduction to the Devout Life,* quite often prominently displayed. Francis de Sales' idea of sanctifying the little things, the ordinary words and actions of everyday life, had somehow captured the French imagination. Good manners were cultivated with exceeding care, and all conversational sins—sharp words, ridicule, aggressiveness—were strictly banned.

With Pierre courtesy had always been quite naturally charity's handmaid. But with him courtesy was likewise truth, and truth sometimes must listen to the unspoken meanings that lie beneath the mere sounds of words. His own manners were so correct, yet so unobtrusive, that others could never properly describe them. For base display and vain pride he had no use at all!

He had known many persons whose fortunes had passed from better to worse. Occasionally, it happened the other way. Once a lady he had known for some time in very limited circumstances suddenly became rich. She kept urging Pierre to pay her a visit. Finally, she was so insistent, and he was so polite, that he went.

She was delighted to have a chance to show off her new house, her furniture, her jewels, even her carriages and costly dresses. But when she brought out the intricately wrought silver tray bearing cards left by socially prominent callers, he could remain silent no longer.

She had been asking over and over, "How do you like all this?"

His reply was not the expected one.

"Oh, Madame, does all this make you very happy?" he asked, looking around the expensively furnished room.

It was an awkward moment. She could not answer, for

Toussaint was one person to whom you could never lie.

In addition, he had a way of sprinkling humor, like a rare titillating spice, over his ordinary conversations. Sometimes it came out in the most unexpected places, which made it all the more delightful. People were always impressed by his good taste and unerring sense of the fitness of things. Just as striking, perhaps the same perception in silhouette, was his sense of disproportion. It could often lead to laughter.

Once when he was ill in bed, a friend dropped in to see him and found him lying, somewhat uncomfortably, with the full glare of the afternoon sun in his face.

"Shall I close the shutter?" she offered.

"Oh no, thank you, Madame," was his quick answer, "for then I shall be too black!"

A strange thing to joke about perhaps, but Pierre was notably unselfconscious about the color of his skin. If he referred to it at all, it was usually in a casual or humorous way. Everyone could see clearly that Pierre's dignity as a son of God had been in no way affected by his being a black man. He never forgot that he had been so created, nor did he wish anyone else to forget it. Still, his special gifts did not always spare him from the blunders and blindness of others. He enjoyed an unusual reputation, but he also lived in a very real world, a world where slavery was widely accepted and exploitation of his race by white men was not outlawed.

It was Pierre's way never to emphasize differences or disagreements. He accepted them and went on from there. By taking everyone else upon an individual and unbiased plane, he quietly imposed the same obligation upon them. Usually, but not, of course, always.

Rarely is the curtain drawn back on those painful moments that surely would have embittered other men. The cursed blade of prejudice must have seared his keen and sensitive mind. But from the rock of his charity it glanced off harmlessly.

One of his black friends once remarked on the irony of the situation.

> *My dear old companion:*
> *Thanks to your regular habits and your fervent prayers, you are still in good health, and I hear very prosperous. But you are still a black man.*
> *You may indeed change your condition— but you will always remain black. Do they mistake you for a white man, that you have a passport everywhere? No. It is because you perceive and follow the naked truth.*
> *Many think that a black skin prevents us from seeing and understanding good from evil. What fools! I have conversed with you at night when it was dark, and I have forgotten that you were not white. The next morning when I saw you, I said to myself, Is this the black man I heard talk last night? Courage! Let them think as they please. Continue to learn, since one may learn always, and communicate your wisdom and experience to those who need it.*

Sometimes on his walks around New York, Pierre had to look quite openly at the ugly face of discrimination. Once he met this on the very doorstep of St. Patrick's Cathedral.

It was the summer of 1842. The young usher, whose name no one apparently remembers, made his insulting remark right there, in front of the altar, so to speak.

It was a highly embarrassing situation for the cathedral authorities. Pierre was an outstanding member of the Catholic community, entitled to every respect, even to special honor, because of his unusual piety, generosity to the church and charity to all.

Louis F. Binsse, president of the board of trustees of St. Patrick's, undertook to make the apology. Binsse was also a Saint Domingue refugee and of course Pierre had been for many years a dear friend of the Binsse family. Here is the letter, dated August 24, 1842.

> *It would be difficult for me to express to you the grief which has been caused me, by the insult which you have received in the Lord's house. It has given me all the more pain, because, wishing to have order in the Church, it was I who begged this gentleman to be one of the masters of ceremony. This young man is truly very repentant for it, and he has been reprimanded most severely by several of the Trustees.*
>
> *Everybody knows, my dear Toussaint, that if God by His will, has created you as well as your good wife, with a black skin, by His grace He has made your hearts and souls as white as snow. While many others (and you know them well) to whom God has given a white skin, having repulsed this same grace, have made their souls, and hearts also, as black as coal.*
>
> *You have been disgusted, my dear friend, by such an insult. I can well believe it. I should have been so, as much as you, and perhaps more than you, because you are human and I also. Our divine Master is the only One, Who, insulted, beaten with rods and crucified, submitted Himself with meekness to the will of His Father, when He could, by the breath of His mouth, have crushed His executioners.*
>
> *What ought we to do then, my dear Toussaint? Imitate Him as much as our weakness and His grace will permit us to do. If by our weakness we resent insult,*

by His grace it should be forgotten. For my part, I should
find myself more at ease, seated in the house of the Lord
between you and your wife, and the good Cabresse,
than beside many other persons whose skin is as white
as satin. In the house of the Lord there is no distinction.
God looks at the heart, but never at the color of the skin.
These are the sentiments of all the Trustees, and of
him who is most sincerely your friend.

Louis F. Binsse.

"The good Cabresse" was evidently a black woman who made her home with the Toussaints. She is referred to very often in Pierre's letters, but never identified. Whether she was a friend or relative of Juliette's, or one of the former slave women from the Bérard plantation we do not know. Juliette's mother Claudine Gaston did live at Reade Street for many years, and a brother, Joseph Gaston, stayed with them from time to time.

Some may ask: Why was Pierre not more militant for the cause of racial justice? It was not his way. His victories were won in a more subtle and perhaps even more effective campaign. Nowadays social justice is often sought by an emphasis on controversial points. Pierre studiously avoided them, and so gained a powerful influence over the minds of those who met him.

One day a Catholic lady who was visiting the Schuylers told Pierre she would like to attend St. Peter's on Sunday morning. She asked if she might have a place in his pew.

"Certainly, Madame, you shall be accommodated," he replied.

Mrs. Schuyler went with her guest to Barclay Street that Sunday before Mass. There was Toussaint, faithful to his promise, waiting courteously for them by the door. He took the visitor to the pew of a Madame Depau, which happened to be vacant.

"But I expected to sit in your pew, Toussaint," the surprised lady remonstrated.

"No, Madame," he answered with dignity, "that would not be proper."

For those of his race, he showed a constant solicitude which took always a very practical and constructive form. Once he received an invitation from a "committee of French gentlemen of color" to become an honorary member of a mutual benevolent society, the *"Frères réunis pour se sécourir en cas de Maladie et Mortalité."*

One of his many avocations was his unofficial employment bureau. He was often called upon to hire servants for the various households he visited, and he never left without exchanging a few words with the domestic staff. They were always certain of his interest and sympathy.

Toussaint used to say of himself, contritely, that he had been born with a quick temper, and would always have to contend with it. Undoubtedly this was so. His reactions were invariably fast and penetrating. Yet his self-command and forbearance were enough that no one but himself ever suffered for it.

"I never heard him speak ill of anyone," a close friend claimed. "If he could say no good, he was silent. Even those who were ungrateful to him met with no angry rebuke. It seemed to be his object to forget all injuries."

On September 15, 1842, Pierre took his now slower way up Greenwich Street, towards the law offices of David C. Colden and George Wilkes. As usual, he was thinking of those he loved. It was a routine matter, the drawing up of a will. Pierre was one who always planned things, and thought out problems before they occurred. His plans seemed to have a singular rationality, and they always seemed to work out well.

In all the world there is nothing so dull as a legal form. Strangely, a profession which deals wholesale with human passion has a language that is wrung dry of any feeling. It is rare indeed that one learns much of a man's personality from his legal papers.

But Pierre felt that the document should be something more than a cold disposition of his goods. Hours passed in the office of Colden and Wilkes that day as Pierre dipped his pen again and again, thoughtfully, covering page after page . . . casting over the hackneyed phrases of the law a strange illumination, the bright radiance of a direct communication from the heart.

> *It was the holy will of God [he wrote] to take from me my beloved adopted daughter Euphemia and I submitted to the blow, with faith in the wisdom of my Heavenly Father . . . But then especially did I appreciate the friendship and sympathy of my two friends Catherine Cruger (who has finished her life of constant benevolence and disinterestedness) and Mary Anne Schuyler, now of the City of New York.*
>
> *Their friendship for many years has been more to me than that of any others, though there are many others whose regard I highly value and appreciate, and I determined after my Euphemia's death that when my estate should no longer be required by my beloved wife Juliette or her Mother, it should pass to the benefit of their children to whom I have been known from their infancies.*

He paused, thinking of the little Philip, Mary Anne's grandson, great-grandson of General Schuyler and of Alexander Hamilton. Even to one who loved all children, this child was special. Pierre tried to picture Philip grown up, a young man in whom the traditions of two famous families would meet. Pierre loved him so much that he intended leaving Philip the greater share of his estate "in order to afford to said Philip the best advantages of education and instruction, so far exceeding in importance the accumulation of property."

But he felt this must be explained, so he added one more paragraph:

> *It was once my will, before it pleased Almighty God to remove him from this world to higher duties, that this part of my estate should be enjoyed by William Sawyer Schuyler, the eldest son of my friends Philip J. Schuyler and Mary Anne Schuyler, as upon him I had placed my warmest and deepest love. But my Heavenly Father has seen it good to call his pure spirit to His own immediate presence, and I now wish to be remembered by his family as one whose heart embraced them all.*
>
> *I pray that Philip may live to equal the virtue, truth and kindness of heart which won for his departed uncle, William, the love of all on whom his smile of gladness fell. . .*

As the years drew in about him, Pierre must have felt the sweetness of memories of times long past. Fifty-eight years had passed since the day he had stepped ashore in New York. The little post-Revolutionary town of thirty thousand souls had become a metropolis of over a million persons.

Even the bitterness of Euphemia's death had been softened.

It had been a crushing denial, for she, more than anyone else on earth, had possessed his heart. Slowly faith, hope and charity had taken the memory of the delicate child and given it the fragrance of unworldly peace. He knew she was with God, and happy.

He had retired more and more from his heavy schedule of work. His needs and those of Juliette were fewer. But for some time he had been saving money in the hope of buying a home on Reade Street where he had always lived. The house he wanted, put up for sale by a John Mills of Jamaica, was too expensive. Mr. Mills' price was $6000. Pierre's limit was $5000. Eventually he found a place within his means at 144 Franklin Street. This was a few blocks north and west of his former address, and had become a rather fashionable area after the fire of 1855.

The City Directory of 1845 shows an entry:

> *Peter Toussaint, home 144 Franklin Street; shop 141 Canal Street.*

It was a pleasant house, beautifully furnished and appointed, and, like all of Juliette's handiwork, exceptional in taste, neatness and artistic arrangement.

As one of the original benefactors of the French church of St. Vincent de Paul, Pierre always received formal notice of all events taking place there, although of course he was still a parishioner of St. Peter's. It gave him great happiness when in 1846 he saw the announcement of the opening of a school for black children in the church basement.

Prospectus

The Rev. M. LaFont has the honor of announcing to the Colored families of this city, that he will open, on the 1st of September next, an English and French School for Young Girls, in the basement of the Church of Saint Vincent de Paul, Canal Street, under the direction of Mrs. Mary Ligneau.

The Catholic Religion is the one professed, however, without exercising any violence over the mind of the children of other denominations. The Course of Instruction will comprise a thorough inculcation of the French and English Languages, Writing, Arithmetic, Geography, History, etc., and the different styles of Needle Work.

The French and English School for Colored Boys, which was opened on the 10th of May last, will be re-opened, in the basement of the same Church, on the 1st of September next. The Course of Instruction will comprise the study of French, English, and Latin Languages, grammatically; Writing, Arithmetic, Geography, History, etc.

Hours For Both Schools

In the morning, from 9 to 11 o'clock.
In the afternoon, from 2 to 4.

Conditions
No children admitted under six years of age.

*First class	$3 per quarter, payable in advance.*
*Second class	$2 per quarter, payable in advance.*
*Third class	$1 per quarter, payable in advance.*

*Parents who cannot comply with the above conditions,
are invited, however, to present their children.*

New York, August 22nd, 1846.

Chapter 23

The Morning Eternal

No," Pierre had said often to himself, like a man losing an argument, "Juliette is much younger than myself. She is strong, very strong. Just now she is nervous, but she will soon be better."

Now he could say it no more. Day after day passed, and she grew no better. Her illness was diagnosed as cancer. They both knew by now how serious it was.

Tonight, as every night, he knelt as best he could with his lame knee in the little oratory he had fixed up between Juliette's room and his. He had assembled there many beautiful symbols of the Faith his friends had given him: the rosary sent by Sarah Anne Moore, sister of Nicholas Fish Moore, President of Columbia University " . . . made up of a fruit from either Mecca or Mount Thabor and . . . consecrated by being laid on the Holy Sepulchre at Jerusalem." And there was the sprig of olives she had sent him from Rome. He had many mementoes from priests, expressions of their gratitude for his charities to them. All these beautiful objects had helped to sustain him in time of trouble. But this night his eyes clung to the plain crucifix hanging before the prie-dieu.

Juliette slept now, or pretended to sleep. Sometimes she lay with closed eyes and prayed, not for herself, but for him. She saw with other eyes, those of the spirit, that he knelt there night after night.

"His only comfort—the cross," she thought, and an anguish deeper than illness held her tightly. "Soon he will be alone, poor Toussaint!"

In those hours he strove again to see in the hand that stripped him the gesture of a benefactor. Could he finally comprehend that Juliette's leaving him would complete a precious work started by Almighty God long ago? One by one, they must all go, all whom he loved so much. All his life, love had drawn him by compassion to the needs of others. Now love drew him by the agony of loneliness to itself.

Their life together had been one of unbroken companionship and mutual charity to all men. As for Juliette, she could hardly remember a time before she had known him.

He had long since faced the end. Over and over the old man, bleak and desolate, had asked into the great silence,

"Is it not strange, Lord, that she should go first, and I be left here alone?"

But his heart held the answer all the time—a homely phrase, the explanation that shook him as the sudden stormwinds of the tropics had shaken the suppliant palms, "It is the will of God."

Juliette died on May 14, 1851.

In his peculiar delicacy he requested that no white persons follow her body to its burial. Whether it remained in St.

Patrick's cemetery is not altogether certain, for the New York City records state cryptically "Removed from city."

After that Pierre turned back haltingly to what was left of the life he had had. Again the streets of the city would know his step, now slow and dispirited, as he continued on his rounds, to the sick, the poor, and those who through the years had come to expect him each day. He always brought with him, instead of the hairdressing tools of former days, a few flowers. It was a custom he had. A token of loyalty. A little tribute of beauty to those who were left.

But he was very tired.

"Do get into an omnibus, Toussaint," someone said to him thoughtlessly.

"I cannot," he replied patiently. "They will not let me!"

For though time had bent his tall frame, bowing it and stooping it, it had not altered the color of his face. That was still black.

It was a year later, in May, 1852, that Fanny Montpensier, faithful correspondent who had addressed so many letters to the Toussaints, wrote Pierre a final letter.

> Let us renew our courage in the sight of the Cross
> of [our] Divine Master, particularly in this beautiful
> month of May, so sad for you and for me. It is true, since
> it recalls to us so many sad memories, but beautiful,
> inasmuch as it bears the lovely name of Mary, to whom
> it is so particularly and so generally consecrated. . . .
> Let us hope that this will be for us a month of grace
> and also of perfect happiness for your dear Juliette.

Fanny closed on a note singularly fitting. Juliette's frequent little offerings had helped in the building of the Oblate Sisters' chapel. Now she would be remembered there.

Father Director of the Oblate Sisters will say Mass on
Wednesday the 12th for her, and the Sisters will offer up
their Communions as well for her on this particular day.
I would have had Mass said on the 11th, but it could
not be said in the Chapel of St. Frances . . . and since I
desired that it be said there, I was obliged to wait until
Wednesday.

Fanny had always been particular about details. Some might have said she was hard to please. Juliette had often joked with her cousin about her zealous promotion of the Sisters' cause.

"You want to pull everyone into Heaven with you!" Juliette had written. And she was right.

In all the years they had never seen him so changed. With Juliette's death, something was broken in Pierre that would never again be whole. And through the break the years rushed in, the terrible, terrible burden which he had borne so long. Eight Popes had reigned during his lifetime—eighty-seven years.

Juliette was gone. Euphemia too. Indeed it seemed sometimes as if the child had never been more than a dream, a bright and fragrant flower, its petals delicate, paper-thin. Aurore Bérard. Mary Anne Schuyler. Catherine Cruger. All the old true friends.

He bowed his head, and wrote again, on a form coldly legal:

Though the pleasure of my Heavenly Father has
taken from me my beloved wife, Juliette, and her

mother, Claudine Gaston, and thus all the provisions of
my said will have become inoperative as to them . . .

He was the last, and responsible to the end, must act
accordingly.

. . . yet it is most congenial to my feelings to have the
assurance of my deep interest and affection in these
now departed ones, as I made them when they were the
objects of my daily concern and care. . . .

He arranged to leave $100.00 to Father Quinn, his pastor,
for his own personal use, asking the prayers of this good man.
And to St. Peter's Church, another $100.00 for Masses for
the soul of Pierre Toussaint, whenever that should become
appropriate.

Now he awaited only the will of his Heavenly Father
concerning himself. That next winter he went so slowly along
to St. Peter's, it seemed he would never arrive at the church.
His health was now obviously failing rapidly, yet everyone saw
him continuing his custom of over sixty years, through snow
and ice and wintry winds, morning after morning making
his slow and feeble passage to God's house. Surely in sixty
years of mornings, cold and gray, heavy and humid, there
had been enough tests of faith to prove a man's fitness for the
morning eternal. But Pierre, we know, was faithfulness itself.
Nothing could have spoken more clearly of what his life had
been than to see him as he was now, still persevering against
great physical hardship in his daily walk to Barclay Street.
Later in the day, his ancient frame, bent with years, would
be seen en route to some distant part of town on a visit of
charity.

Spring came again to the city. Peter Stuyvesant's wonderful
pear tree—the last hardy survivor of his Bowery Farm—

bloomed again at the corner of Second Avenue and 13th Street. But for Pierre there would be no other springs. By this time he could no longer walk to St. Peter's, so he sat at home, plunged in deep depression at this deprivation. But this was a passing trial, a sadness that soon disappeared, leaving only peace.

A Protestant friend had asked during this period:

"Shall I ask a priest to come and see you? Perhaps you would like to go to confession—perhaps it would relieve you to talk to him."

After a long moment, Toussaint answered.

"A priest is a man; when I am at confession, I confess to God; when I stand up, I see a man before me."

Mary Anne Schuyler's sister, Hannah Lee, who became Pierre's first biographer, went to call on him in his Franklin Street home.

> *When I last saw Toussaint, I perceived that his days were numbered, that he stood on the borders of the infinite. He was feeble, but sitting in an arm-chair, clad in his dressing- gown, and supported by pillows. A more perfect representation of a gentleman I have seldom seen. His head was strewn with the "blossoms of the grave."*
>
> *When he saw me he was overcome by affecting remembrances, for we had last met at the funeral obsequies of the friend so dear to him [Mary Anne Schuyler]. He trembled with emotion, and floods of tears fell from his eyes.*
>
> *"It is all so changed! so changed!" said he. "So lonely!"*
>
> *He was too weak to converse, but his mind was filled with images of the past. . . .*

The next day I saw him again, and took leave of him to see him no more in this world. It was with deep feeling that I quitted his house—that house where I had seen the beings he dearly loved collected.

It was a bright summer morning, the last of May; the windows were open, and looked into the little garden, with its few scattered flowers. There was nobody now I had ever seen there, but himself— the aged solitary man.

Eliza Hamilton Schuyler went to see him faithfully during the last days. She told of these visits.

Toussaint was in bed today; he says it is now the most comfortable place for him, or as he expressed it in French, "Il ne peut pas être mieux."

He was drowsy and indistinct, but calm, cheerful, and placid—the expression of his countenance truly religious. He told me he had received the last Communion, for which he had been earnest, and mentioned that two Sisters of Charity had been to see him, and prayed with him.

He speaks of the excellent care he receives—of his kind nurse (she is a white woman)—and said, "All is well."

He sent me away when he was tired, by thanking me.

She went every day now.

I saw him on Sunday; he was very low, and neither spoke nor noticed me. On Monday, when I entered, he had revived a little, and looking up, said,

"Dieu avec moi" — *God is with me.*

When I asked him if he wanted anything, he replied with a smile, "Rien sur la terre— " Nothing on earth.

223

As far as we can know, these words were his last, He died, four days later, on Thursday, at twelve o'clock. It was June 30, 1853.

There was no pain, no visible agony. Just a barely perceptible alteration from his extreme weakness. His soul had long been ready; his body was too tired to protest.

He left not one living relative, at least none that were known, although in his will he had made provision to care for any who might be found, either in America or in Haiti. Yet St. Peter's Church was crowded on the day of his funeral with persons, both white and black, who had revered him. Perhaps there were men present who had been orphan boys living in his home. No doubt there were some he had nursed during sickness, some he had aided with money, once or many times, others he had consoled in their sorrows, and surely some who had first known him at the Prince Street orphanage. The nuns were there, the Sisters of Charity. The people whose homes he had visited daily for so long, the sons and daughters of his old-time customers, to whom he had been much more than Toussaint the coiffeur. As one of them put it: "He dressed my hair for my first Communion; he dressed it for my wedding, and for christenings, for balls and parties; at burials, in sickness and in trouble, he was always there."

Eliza Schuyler was one of those for whom Toussaint spanned a lifetime. She was present at St. Peter's that morning, and she wrote her impressions down.

> *I went to town on Saturday, to attend Toussaint's funeral. High Mass, incense, candles, rich robes, and solemn music, were there. The Church gave all it could give, to prince or noble. The priest, his friend, Mr.*

*Quinn, made a most interesting address. He did not
allude to his color, and scarcely to his station; it seemed
as if his virtues as a man and a Christian had absorbed
all other thoughts. A stranger would not have suspected
that a black man, of his humble calling, lay in the midst
of us. He said, though no relative is left to mourn for
him, yet many present would feel that they had lost
one who always had wise counsel for the rich, words of
encouragement for the poor, and all would be grateful
for having known him.*

*The aid he had given to the late Bishop Fenwick of
Boston, to Father Power of our city, to all the Catholic
institutions, was dwelt upon at large. How much I have
learnt of his charitable deeds, which I had never known
before!*

Father Quinn expressed his opinion of his late parishioner
very forthrightly:

*There are few left among the clergy superior to him
in devotion and zeal for the Church and for the glory of
God; among laymen, none.*

When Juliette was buried, Toussaint had requested that
none of their white friends follow her remains. His wish was
now remembered. No one followed after the coffin when it
was carried from the church. But in St. Patrick's churchyard,
when Pierre's body was laid down to its peace, there were
many who stood around the grave.

There was one more thing to be done. Pierre had
appointed the Schuyler brothers, George Lee and Robert, his
executors. They went to Franklin Street in that capacity to
put his belongings in order. On the desk lay some papers,
the last ones on which Toussaint had been working. It was

a meticulous account of his last collection for the orphans, the one he had been taking up just before he was stricken. The money was there too, all ready to be handed over for the children he had never forgotten.

They took down his metal crucifix from the wall. On the back were fastened little slips of paper with the words: "To Toussaint from a grateful priest!"

EPILOGUE

Now he was gone. The venerable man whom everyone recognized, to whom most bowed in spirit as they passed. The tireless walker of sixty-six years was missing from New York streets, and that minute silence, the absence of a well-known footfall, was noted in, of all places, the newspaper offices. The hectic clackety-clack of typewriters had not yet come to the city-rooms, so perhaps in those sultry, early-summer days in 1855, with the pen scratching along in a somewhat pedestrian fashion, it was even possible to reflect on what was going into the finely printed columns of that day's edition.

On Saturday, July 2, two morning papers in the city carried this story:

> *Pierre Toussaint, whose funeral will take place this morning, at ten o'clock, from St. Peter's Church, Barclay Street, was born in the servitude of St. Domingo, and, in devoted attendance upon his mistress in her flight from that island, arrived in this city in 1787. Here the former dependent became the support of the unfortunate lady, and her most disinterested friend until her death.*

*The occupation of ladies' hair-dresser gave him
admission to the houses of the influential families of
that day, and his good manners, unusual discrimination
of character, and high sense of propriety insured him
the countenance, courtesy, and esteem of all to whom
he was admitted, and the confidence and friendship of
many to whom the excellence of his life and character
was more intimately known. All knew his general worth,
but few were acquainted with the generous qualities of
his heart, and with those principles of disinterested and
genuine kindness which governed his daily conduct.*

*His charity was of the efficient character which did
not content itself with a present relief of pecuniary
aid, but which required time and thought by day and
night, and long watchfulness and kind attentions at the
bedside of the sick and the departing. Thus goodness
springing from refined and elevated principle, and
from a sense of religious duty, which never permitted
him to omit a most scrupulous compliance with all the
requirements of his faith, formed the prominent feature
of his character, and made his life a constant round of
acts of kindness and sympathy.*

*By such a life, governed by such principles of
integrity, charity and religion, Toussaint secured to
himself the respect, esteem, and friendship of many of
our first citizens; and though death has made the circle
small in which he had moved, there are yet remaining
many who remembered his excellence and worth with
the kindest appreciation.*

S.

Perhaps this was written by one of the Schuylers as a last
loving tribute to the worth of a good friend.

Others tried to explain his virtues. Everyone knew him, yet no one could put him on paper exactly as he was to them. Toussaint was such a familiar figure—a symbol, almost—yet he seemed to slip out of pen-hold time and again as they sought to sum him up. And this was very natural, for he had always shunned publicity.

The New York *Post* recounted some anecdotes of his charities:

> *Toussaint is spoken of by all who knew him as a man of the warmest and most active benevolence, the gentlest temper, and the most courteous and graceful, yet wholly unassuming manners. The successive pastors of St. Peter's Church had all the same opinion of him, and it is said that, when the present pastor came to bury him, he observed that he had not such a man left among his congregation. It would be worth the while of any one who knew him well, to give in a brief memoir some anecdotes of a life which was, throughout, so shining an example of goodness. . . .*

Henry J. Tuckerman, whose popular novels were being serialized in newspapers in those days, tried his hand — and a very literary hand it was — in an article in the New York *Home Journal*:

> *Died on Thursday, June 30th, at his residence in this city, Pierre Toussaint, in the eighty-seventh year of his age.*
>
> *We cannot allow this brief announcement to form the sole record of one whose example is a higher vindication of his race, or rather a nobler testimony to the beauty and force of character, than all the works of fiction that studious invention ever conceived.*

Pierre Toussaint for more than sixty years had been
the most respected and beloved Negro in New York. He
came here in 1787, with his mistress . . . He soon began
to exercise his rare talent as a hair-dresser, and became
indispensable to the ladies of New York, and their
children. A very few of the brides, whose tresses he so
daintily arrayed, yet survive; and as long as any of them
lived, Pierre paid them regular visits, and was always
certain of a kind reception. He supported his beloved
mistress, not only in comfort, but luxury, when her
means failed, until the day of her death.

Meantime, he had associated himself with all the best
families. The wives and daughters loved to listen to his
tropical reminiscences, or his cheerful comments on the
news of the day, as he adorned their heads for the evening
party; and the children delighted to put themselves under
his kindly hands when the time came for a hair-cutting.
Pierre was thus busy from morning to night. . . .

After the death of his mistress he married, and was
enabled to purchase a very good home in Franklin
Street. He retired from business with an adequate
fortune, and thenceforth devoted himself to social and
benevolent duty. His relations in the former respect were
three-fold; first, to his cherished lady friends and their
families, whom he had attended in youth, and towards
whom he exhibited a disinterested and loyal attachment,
which seemed to belong to a past age or a different
country, so unique and touching was its manifestation;
second, to the French population of New York, to
whom he was attached by early association and native
language; and thirdly, to his own race. . . .

By these so widely different classes, Pierre was
both respected and beloved. He moved among them

*in a way peculiarly his own. He possessed a sense of
the appropriate, a self-respect, and a uniformity of
demeanor, which amounted to genius. No familiarity
ever made him forget what was due to his superiors,
and prosperity and reputation never hardened his heart
towards the less favored of his own class.*

*For sixty years he attended Mass at six in the
morning, as punctual as a clock, until prostrated
by illness. His days and nights were given to visits,
ministrations to the sick, attendance upon the bereaved,
and attempts to reform the erring and console the
afflicted. . . . Often strangers paused to look with curiosity
and surprise upon the singular tableau presented in
Broadway of the venerable Negro, with both his hands
clasped in greeting by a lady high in the circles of fashion
or birth, and to watch the vivid interest of both, as they
exchanged inquiries for each other's welfare.*

*The last time I saw Pierre, he was seated among a
group of mourners, beside the coffin of a lady venerated
for years in the highest social sphere of the city. [Mary
Anne Schuyler.] She was almost the last tie that bound
him to the past. He had visited her daily for thirty years,
and brought his offering of flowers; and there he sat,
with his white head bowed in grief, and every line of
his honest sable face wet with tears. It was a beautiful
homage to watch—a beautiful instance of what may
be the disinterested relation between the exalted and
the humble— when the genius of character and the
sentiment of religion bring them thus together.*

*Pierre was buried in the Cathedral Churchyard
beside his wife and adopted child; and his funeral was
attended by gentlemen and menials; his death-bed,
soothed by the fairest as well as venerated by the most*

*humble representatives of the wide circle included in his
sympathies and attracted by his worth.*

*Peace to the ashes of good, noble, loyal Pierre
Toussaint!*

An article by Emma Cary appeared in *Ave Maria Magazine*
in 1893. She had known Toussaint in her childhood. She
had grown up in a Protestant home but later on she became
a convert to Catholicism. She remembered Toussaint's
apologetics in her household when she was quite small:

> *His life was so perfect, and he explained the teaching
> of the Church with a simplicity so intelligent and so cou-
> rageous that everyone honored him as a Catholic. He
> would explain our devotion to the Mother of God with
> the utmost clearness, or show the union of the natural
> and supernatural gifts in the priests, or quote our great
> spiritual writers in a way to account best for the faith he
> bore.*

> *When I was young I used to hear Protestants speak
> with reverence of two Catholics — the great Fenelon and
> the humble Toussaint! . . .*

> *I believe Pierre Toussaint to have been a man who
> dwelt above the region of human passions and personal
> interests. He had a strong sense of the dignity of being a
> creature of God, and no outward circumstance of birth,
> of station, or even of bondage, could lessen his interior
> contentment. . . . I believe he never gauged his own mer-
> its by any measure of man's making, but said, like St.
> Francis of Assisi: "What I am in Thy sight, O God! that
> am I, and no more."*

A white man who had roomed with the Toussaints
described their home life:

Such was the even tenor of his way while I lived under his roof, that nothing occurs particularly to my memory. You know there is no being on earth who presents so few prominent and recollectable points as a "perfect gentleman."

If you undertake to describe any such person whom you have ever known, you will find him most indescribable. So it was with Toussaint.

His manners were gentle and courtly—how can this simple statement be expanded into details, so as to give a better idea of them? The most unaffected good humor at all times, the most respectful and polite demeanor without the slightest tincture of servility, the most natural and artless conversation—all this I remember of him, as every one else remembers who knows him; but all his intercourse was so unobtrusive that it is difficult for me to recall anything marked.

I remember how much I was pleased with his deportment and behavior toward his wife. Juliette was a good woman, but unlike Toussaint; she was flesh and blood, while he was possessed of the spirit of one man out of many thousands. I never met with any other of his race who made me forget his color. Toussaint, for his deportment, discretion, good sense, and entire trustworthiness and fidelity might have discharged creditably all the functions of a courtier or privy councillor. His politeness, which was uniform, never led you for a moment to suspect his sincerity; it was the natural overflow, the inevitable expression of his heart, and you no more thought of distrusting it than of failing to reciprocate it, and I cannot imagine that any one could offer him an indignity.

A few weeks after the funeral the *New York Home Journal* spoke of Pierre again, announcing briefly that "a Boston lady" was about to publish his biography.

The book appeared very shortly. Its author was Hannah Lee, the sister of Mary Anne Schuyler. She registered her *Memoirs of Pierre Toussaint* in the Library of Congress less than six months after his death. It is to this little volume that we are indebted for much of the material of this work, and of its authenticity there can be no doubt. We may even conjecture that Mary Anne Schuyler herself, an old woman but still a Schuyler with a debt to history, was planning to write an account of her dear "St. Pierre." At any rate she had collected the material, for it was from her extensive notes that Hannah Lee wrote. Another striking detail: it seems that most of the work on the *Memoirs* had been done before Pierre himself died, for the obituary notices quoted above appear as an Appendix to the book, a last-minute addition from newspapers "a few days ago." This was a further testimony to Pierre's reputation among those who knew him best.

There, in Hannah Lee's book, rested the legend of Pierre. At least for a time. It was kept alive, however, in the households of families who had known him; the Binsses, for instance, and the LaFarges, and of course the Schuylers. Stories of him were handed down to children who often heard his name spoken with reverence, and could not help but realize his like could come no more. And so the legend did not die. And in the attics of some of these old homes, on a rainy afternoon, one might run across the dusty volume, bearing in the front the likeness of a dignified black man, very proper in his old-fashioned cravat.

A trunk full of Pierre's letters and papers, most of them bearing witness directly or indirectly to his innumerable charities, was found by his executors. They were preserved with care by the Schuyler family, who kept them intact for fifty years.

In 1903 Georgina Schuyler, Mary Anne's granddaughter, presented the Toussaint papers to New York's "First Citizen," John Shaw Billings, director of the recently organized New York Public Library. The collection consisted of five boxes, now on file in the manuscript division, containing over two thousand pages of letters, notes, invitations, church programs, and records of money collected for the Catholic orphans of New York.

Meantime, in Mott Street, time and the weather and man's forgetfulness dealt oblivion to the little cemetery now submerged in a teeming city. Inside its carefully kept gates, it is true, the grass always seemed greener, jewel-bright in contrast to the dingy, sagging tenements which surrounded St. Patrick's churchyard. Very few ever stopped to notice.

St. Patrick's had become simply a parish church, its gracious beauty mellowed with age, its interior dignity unruffled by lesser status. Uptown, at Fifth Avenue and 51st Street, it was now the new St. Patrick's Cathedral that caused the tourist to pause in wonder. Nothing in the guidebooks reminded him that around the old cathedral, far downtown, the remains of some thirty thousand of New York's early Catholics were laid.

Eventually a young seminarian, now Father Charles H. McTague of Fairview, New Jersey, was inspired by the Catholic Interracial Council of New York to try to discover among the worn and illegible stones of the graveyard the one marking Pierre's grave. It was a perplexing task. He systematically plotted the original grave rows one by one, and by comparison of legible stones with available records he located the place where Toussaint's grave should be. After close study of that stone, the faintest trace of the name could be seen.

Pierre—the name of rock written on rock—and both subject to matter's peculiar destiny, decay! All that remained here was carved in frail man's memory, the reverence for a great personality.

It was to honor this great personality that Francis Cardinal Spellman, Archbishop of New York, went to the almost obliterated grave site in 1951 and solemnly blessed a plaque placed there by the John Boyle O'Reilly Society for Interracial Justice. Again, on June 29, 1953, Pierre Toussaint was honored by a pontifical Mass of thanksgiving celebrated in his memory at Old St. Peter's on Barclay Street. On the outer wall of the church a bronze tablet commemorating one whose presence had done honor to God's house was blessed by Bishop Joseph Donahue before the many clergymen, civic officials, citizens of all ranks who had come to pay tribute to the noble Toussaint.

Pierre's lifetime had spanned almost a century. To him, years must have meant little after a while. They came and went, while love remained. Longevity, a bequest from his tribal ancestors, had given him a rare perspective on human affairs. And so after death, a hundred years passed by and everything seemed different, except for him. People spoke lengthily of social justice, sometimes forgetting love. And New York had grown into a great stronghold of Catholicism, churches, schools, hospitals, orphanages—all taken for granted, the countless little cornerstones of Pierre's pioneer charities quite unnoticed. Through the shriek of traffic and the grinding, smoky pace of progress, prayers ascended continually from New York to Heaven, a route well worn by Toussaint long ago.

ACKNOWLEDGMENTS

The authors' thanks are due to many persons and libraries for the aid given in the necessary research. Father John LaFarge, S.J., George K. Hunton, Richard Condon, Patrick J. Mullaney and Schuyler Warren of the New York Catholic Interracial Council must be especially mentioned.

The authors had recourse to many libraries; to the Manuscript Division and Schomburg collection as well as to the general section of the New York Public Library, to the Boston Athenaeum, the Yale University Library, Bibliotheque Nationale and French Archives, Paris, The New York Historical Society and the library of the National Geographic Society.

The priests of Old St. Peter's Church, Barclay Street, New York, graciously put the parish records at the writers' disposal. The Oblate Sisters of Providence in Baltimore supplied valuable information. John Glennon assisted in technical problems of microfilming and photostating manuscript material. Anne Marie Stokes helped with the French translations. Elizabeth Herbermann of the New York Catholic Historical Society obtained valuable background material as did Samuel Newberry and Richard Shafter. Mary Ellen Evans and Robert McDonald contributed much-needed encouragement.

Lastly a word of thanks to that mysterious angel who opened so many doors in a research task that oftentimes seemed impossible.

Note to the Reader

Events in this book are based on and inspired by the childhood memories of Marian Moore Wolfe. But memory is a funny thing. Sometimes it is only a snapshot of a rich experience. To enrich the snapshot, I also interviewed others who grew up during the 1930s on Fontana farms (in Southern California) and mining communities of the Sierras in Calaveras and Tuolumne counties. I've read historical accounts, newspapers, books, and when possible visited the locations found in the stories. Where memory faltered, I attempted to fill in with some of these other resources, and when a picture was still incomplete, I used my imagination. So, although this collection of stories is based on oral history, details surrounding Marian's memory were compressed, expanded, overlaid, and imagined to bring her experiences more fully alive for the reader.

In October 2006, I showed up on Marian's doorstep, tape recorder in hand, her husband being our matchmaker. He knew she had vivid memories of growing up during the Great